RMEldridge

1

STORY OF JESUS

Jesus, The Master Pilot

With Jesus, the Master Pilot, at the helm of life's
ship, we can rest in perfect assurance that He
will take us safely through the stormiest seas
and bring us to our desired haven.

STORY OF JESUS

By

Ellen G. White

(ADAPTED)

For three generations the material contained in the present volume *Story of Jesus* delighted boys and girls under the title of *Christ Our Saviour*. More than three-quarter million copies of the book under that title were sold. The new book has the same text the old one had, but has more and better pictures. The type has been entirely reset. It is the hope of the publishers that the boys and girls of today will find as much delight and pleasure in reading *Story of Jesus* as their parents and grandparents found in *Christ Our Saviour*.

SOUTHERN PUBLISHING ASSOCIATION
NASHVILLE, TENN.

(PRINTED IN U. S. A.)

Lovingly Presented

to _____

from _____

Preface

THE influence of the earthly life of Jesus our Saviour appears on every feature of nature, in every phase of human experience, in every fact of life. We can never fully realize how deep is the impression, how widespread is the influence, of the life of Jesus of Nazareth. Every blessing of every kind comes to us through that connection between Heaven and earth which was formed when the Lord of glory espoused the cause of a world lost in sin.

The infinite pathos of that story has inspired the pen of the learned and the tongue of the eloquent. But it is best told in childlike language. The wonderful spectacle needs no human coloring. Its glory surpasses the art of men. It shines brightest in its own luster.

In these pages no effort is made toward artificial embellishment. The plain story, as told by one who is moved by a deep sense of the infinite proportions of the subject, has been put into the language of the young. In its simplicity not only does it speak to the hearts of the young, but it meets the desire expressed by us all in the familiar song—

"Tell me the story simply, as to a little child."

May it be received in the same simplicity and purity of faith.　　　　　　　　　　　　　　GEORGE C. TENNEY.

Contents

CONTENTS—Continued

Because the innkeeper could find no room for them, Joseph and Mary had to seek
shelter in a stable. Here Jesus, the Creator of the universe, found a humble welcome
amid the lowing of cattle and bleating of sheep.

The Birth of Jesus

*I*N THE little town of Nazareth, nestled among the hills of Galilee, was the home of Joseph and Mary, who were afterward known as the earthly parents of Jesus.

Now Joseph was of the lineage, or family, of David; and so, when a decree was sent out for the people to be taxed, he had to go to Bethlehem, the city of David, to have his name enrolled. This was a toilsome journey, as people traveled in those times. Mary, who went with her husband, was very weary as she climbed the hill on which Bethlehem stands.

How she longed for a comfortable place in which to rest! But the inns were already full. The rich and proud were well cared for, while these humble travelers had to find rest in a rude building where cattle were sheltered.

Joseph and Mary possessed little of earth's riches, but they had the love of God, and this made them rich in contentment and peace. They were children of the heavenly King, who was about to give them a wonderful honor.

Angels had been watching them while they were on their journey, and when night came on, and they went to rest, they were not left alone. Angels were still with them.

P. THUMANN

All heaven rejoiced at the birth of Jesus, and angel messengers hastened to tell the wondrous news to lowly shepherds as they watched their flocks by night on the Judean hillsides.

There, in that lowly shed, Jesus the Saviour was born and laid in a manger. In that rude cradle lay the Son of the Highest—He whose presence had filled the courts of Heaven with glory.

Before He came to the earth, Jesus was the Commander of the angel hosts. The brightest and most exalted of the sons of the morning heralded His glory at the creation. They veiled their faces before Him as He sat upon His throne. They cast their crowns at His feet, and sang His triumphs as they beheld His greatness.

Yet this glorious Being loved the poor sinner, and took upon Him the form of a servant, that He might suffer and die for us.

Jesus might have remained at the Father's side, wearing the kingly crown and the royal robe; but for our sake He chose to exchange the riches of Heaven for the poverty of earth.

He chose to leave His station of high command, to leave the angels who loved Him. The adoration of the heavenly throng He chose to exchange for mockery and abuse by wicked men. From love to us, He accepted a life of hardship and a death of shame.

All this Christ did to show how much God loves us. He lived on earth to show how we may honor God by obedience to His will. He did this so that by following His example we may at last dwell with Him in His heavenly home.

The priests and rulers among the Jews were not ready to welcome Jesus. They knew that the Saviour was soon to come, but they expected Him to be a mighty king who would make them rich and great. They were too proud to think of the Messiah as being a helpless child.

So when Christ was born, God did not reveal it to them. He sent the glad news to some shepherds who kept their flocks on the hills around Bethlehem.

These were good men, and as they watched their sheep by night, they talked together about the promised Saviour, and prayed so earnestly for His coming that God sent bright messengers from His own throne of light to teach them.

"And, lo, the angel of the Lord came upon them, and the glory of the Lord shone round about them: and they were sore afraid.

"And the angel said unto them, Fear not: for, behold, I bring you good tidings of great joy, which shall be to all people. For unto you is born this day in the city of David a Saviour, which is Christ the Lord.

"And this shall be a sign unto you; Ye shall find the babe wrapped in swaddling clothes, lying in a manger.

"And suddenly there was with the angel a multitude of the heavenly host praising God, and saying, Glory to God in the highest, and on earth peace, good will toward men.

"And it came to pass, as the angels were gone away from them into heaven, the shepherds said one to another, Let us now go even unto Bethlehem, and see this thing which is come to pass, which the Lord hath made known unto us.

"And they came with haste, and found Mary, and Joseph, and the babe lying in a manger. And when they had seen it, they made known abroad the saying which was told them concerning this child.

"And all they that heard it wondered at those things which were told them by the shepherds. But Mary kept all these things, and pondered them in her heart." Luke 2:9-19.

"Mine Eyes Have Seen Thy Salvation"

When the infant Jesus was brought to the temple for the dedication service, the aged prophet Simeon praised God for letting him see the promised Messiah before he should die.

PAINTING BY WM. C. T. DOBSON

Jesus Presented in the Temple

*J*OSEPH and Mary were Jews, and followed the customs of their nation. When Jesus was six weeks old, they brought Him to the Lord in the temple at Jerusalem.

This was according to the law which God had given to Israel, and Jesus was to be obedient in all things. So God's own Son, the Prince of Heaven, by His example teaches that we should obey.

Only the first-born son of each family was thus presented at the temple. This ceremony was to keep in memory an event that had taken place long before.

When the children of Israel were slaves in Egypt, the Lord sent Moses to set them free. He bade Moses go to Pharaoh, king of Egypt, and say:

"Thus saith the Lord, Israel is My son, even My firstborn: and I say unto thee, Let My son go, that he may serve Me: and if thou refuse to let him go, behold, I will slay thy son, even thy firstborn." Exodus 4:22, 23.

Moses carried this message to the king. But Pharaoh's

2

answer was, "Who is the Lord, that I should obey His voice to let Israel go? I know not the Lord, neither will I let Israel go." Exodus 5:2.

Then the Lord sent fearful plagues upon the Egyptians. The last of these plagues was the slaying of the first-born son of every family, from that of the king to the lowliest in the land.

The Lord told Moses that every family of the Israelites must kill a lamb, and put some of the blood upon the door-posts of their dwellings.

This was a sign, that the angel of death might *pass over* all the houses of the Israelites, and destroy none but the proud and cruel Egyptians.

This blood of the "Passover" represented to the Jews the blood of Christ. For in due time, God would give His dear Son to be slain as the lamb had been slain; so that all who should believe in Him might be saved from everlasting death. Christ is called our Passover. (1 Corinthians 5:7.) By His blood, through faith, we are redeemed. (Ephesians 1:7.)

So as each family in Israel brought the eldest son to the temple, they were to remember how the children had been saved from the plague, and how all might be saved from sin and eternal death. The child presented at the temple was taken in the arms of the priest, and held up before the altar.

Thus it was solemnly dedicated to God. Then after it was given back to the mother, its name was written in the roll, or book, that contained the names of the first-born of Israel. So all who are saved by Christ's blood will have their names written in the book of life.

Joseph and Mary brought Jesus to the priest as the law required. Every day fathers and mothers were coming with their children, and in Joseph and Mary the priest saw nothing different from many others. They were simply working people.

In the child Jesus he saw only a helpless infant. Little did the priest think that he was then holding in his arms the Saviour of the world, the High Priest of the heavenly temple. But he might have known; for if he had been obedient to God's Word, the Lord would have taught him these things.

At this very time there were in the temple two of God's true servants, Simeon and Anna. Both had grown old in His service, and He showed them things that could not be made known to the proud and selfish priests.

To Simeon had been given the promise that he should not die until he had seen the Saviour. As soon as he saw Jesus in the temple, he knew that this was the promised One.

Upon the face of Jesus there was a soft, heavenly light; and Simeon, taking the child in his arms, praised God, and said:

"Lord, now lettest Thou Thy servant depart in peace, according to Thy word: for mine eyes have seen Thy salvation, which Thou hast prepared before the face of all people; a light to lighten the Gentiles, and the glory of Thy people Israel." Luke 2:29-32.

Anna, a prophetess, "coming in that instant gave thanks likewise unto the Lord, and spake of Him to all them that looked for redemption in Jerusalem." Luke 2:38.

So it is that God chooses humble people to be His wit-

nesses. Often those whom the world calls great are passed
by. Many are like the Jewish priests and rulers.

Many are eager to serve and honor themselves, but think
little about serving and honoring God. Therefore He cannot choose them to tell others of His love and mercy.

Mary, the mother of Jesus, pondered the far-reaching
prophecy of Simeon. As she looked upon the child in her
arms, and recalled what the shepherds of Bethlehem had
said, she was full of grateful joy and bright hope.

Simeon's words called to her mind the prophecy of
Isaiah. She knew that of Jesus were spoken these wonderful words:

"The people that walked in darkness have seen a great
light: they that dwell in the land of the shadow of death,
upon them hath the light shined."

"For unto us a child is born, unto us a Son is given:
and the government shall be upon His shoulder: and His
name shall be called Wonderful, Counsellor, the Mighty
God, the Everlasting Father, the Prince of Peace." Isaiah
9:2, 6.

The Visit of the Wise Men

*G*OD wanted the people to know about the coming of Christ to the earth. The priests should have taught the people to look for the Saviour; but they themselves did not know of His coming.

So God sent angels to tell the shepherds that Christ was born, and where they might find Him.

So, too, when Jesus was presented at the temple, there were those who received Him as the Saviour. God had preserved the lives of Simeon and Anna, and they had the joyful privilege of testifying that Jesus was the promised Messiah.

God meant for others, as well as the Jews, to know that Christ had come. In a country far to the east were wise men who had studied the prophecies concerning the Messiah, and who believed that His coming was near.

The Jews called these men heathen; but they were not idolaters. They were honest men, who wanted to know the truth, and to do the will of God.

God looks upon the heart, and He knew that these men could be trusted. They were in a better condition to receive

21

SEATON SPENCE

The Wise Men were students of both the heavens and the Scriptures. They recognized
in the bright, new star a sign that the Promised One had come to earth, and they
set out at once on the long journey to find Him.

light from Heaven than were the Jewish priests, who were so full of selfishness and pride.

These wise men were philosophers. They had studied the handiwork of God in nature, and had learned to love Him there. They had studied the stars, and knew their movements.

They loved to watch the heavenly bodies in their nightly march. If a new star should be seen, they would welcome its appearance as a great event.

On that night when the angels came to the shepherds of Bethlehem, the wise men had noticed a strange light in the sky. It was the glory which surrounded the angel host.

When this light faded away, they had seen in the heavens what looked like a new star. At once they thought of the prophecy which says, "There shall come a Star out of Jacob, and a Sceptre shall rise out of Israel." Numbers 24:17. Was this star a sign that the Messiah had come? They determined to follow it, and see where it would lead them. It led them into Judea. But when they came near to Jerusalem, the star grew so dim that they could not follow it.

Supposing that the Jews could at once guide them to the Saviour, the wise men went into Jerusalem, and said, "Where is He that is born King of the Jews? For we have seen His star in the east, and are come to worship Him.

"When Herod the king had heard these things, he was troubled, and all Jerusalem with him. And when he had gathered all the chief priests and scribes of the people together, he demanded of them where Christ should be born. And they said unto him, In Bethlehem of Judea: for thus it is written by the prophet." Matthew 2:2-5.

Herod did not like to hear of a king who might some

day take his throne. So he took the wise men by themselves, and asked when they first saw the star. Then he sent them to Bethlehem, saying: "Go and search diligently for the young child; and when ye have found Him, bring me word again, that I may come and worship Him also."

When the wise men heard this, they started again on their journey. "And, lo, the star, which they saw in the east, went before them, till it came and stood over where the young child was.

"When they were come into the house, they saw the young child with Mary His mother, and fell down, and worshiped Him: and when they had opened their treasures, they presented unto Him gifts; gold, and frankincense, and myrrh." Matthew 2:6-11.

The most precious things they had, the wise men brought to the Saviour. In this they set an example for us. Many give presents to their earthly friends, but have none for the heavenly Friend who has given them every blessing. We should not do this. To Christ we should bring the best of all we have—of our time, money, and our love.

We may give to Him by giving to comfort the poor, and to teach people about the Saviour. So we can help to save those for whom He died. Such gifts Jesus blesses.

The Flight Into Egypt

*H*EROD had not been honest in saying that he wanted to go and worship Jesus. He feared that the Saviour would grow up to be a king, and take his kingdom from him.

He wanted to find the child, that he might have Him put to death.

The wise men prepared to return and tell Herod. But the angel of the Lord appeared to them in a dream, and sent them home another way.

"And when they were departed, behold, the angel of the Lord appeareth to Joseph in a dream, saying, Arise, and take the young child and His mother, and flee into Egypt, and be thou there until I bring thee word: for Herod will seek the young child to destroy Him." Matthew 2:13.

Joseph did not wait till morning; he rose at once, and with Mary and the child, started by night on the long journey.

The wise men had given costly presents to Jesus, and in this way God provided for the expenses of the journey and

H. KAULBACH

Mary and Joseph, with little Jesus, escaping into Egypt from the wrath of wicked Herod, stop by the wayside for some refreshment.

their stay in Egypt, until they should return to their own land.

Herod was very angry when he found that the wise men had gone home another way. He knew what God by His prophet had said about Christ's coming.

He knew how the star had been sent as a guide to the wise men. Yet he was determined to destroy Jesus. In his wrath he sent soldiers to kill "all the children that were in Bethlehem, . . . from two years old and under." Matthew 2:16.

How strange that a man should fight against God! What an awful scene this slaying of the innocent children must have been! Herod had before done many cruel things; but his wicked life was soon to end. He died a terrible death.

Joseph and Mary remained in Egypt till after the death of Herod. Then the angel appeared to Joseph, and said, "Arise, and take the young child and His mother, and go into the land of Israel: for they are dead which sought the young child's life." Matthew 2:20.

Joseph had hoped to make his home in Bethlehem, where Jesus was born; but on coming near to Judea, he learned that a son of Herod was reigning in place of his father.

This made Joseph afraid to go there, and he did not know what to do; so God sent an angel to instruct him. Following the directions of the angel, Joseph returned to his old home in Nazareth.

H. J. SINKEL

Jesus set a wonderful example for us all by honoring His parents and thereby also honoring God's holy law.

Child Life of Jesus

*J*ESUS in His childhood lived in a little mountain village. He was the Son of God, and He might have had any place on earth for His home.

He would have been an honor to any place. But He did not go to the homes of rich men or the palaces of kings. He chose to dwell among the poor in Nazareth.

Jesus wants the poor to know that He understands their trials. He has borne all that they have to bear. He can sympathize with them and help them.

Of Jesus in His early years the Bible says, "The child grew, and waxed strong in spirit, filled with wisdom: and the grace of God was upon Him." "And Jesus increased in wisdom and stature, and in favor with God and man." Luke 2:40, 52.

His mind was bright and active. He was of quick understanding, and showed a thoughtfulness and wisdom beyond His years. Yet His ways were simple and childlike, and He grew in mind and body as other children grow.

But Jesus was not in all things like other children. He

always showed a sweet, unselfish spirit. His willing hands were always ready to serve others. He was patient and truthful.

Firm as a rock in standing for the right, He never failed to be gentle and courteous toward all. In His home, and wherever He might be, He was like a cheerful sunbeam.

He was thoughtful and kind toward the aged and the poor, and He showed kindness even to the dumb animals. He would care tenderly for a little wounded bird, and every living thing was happier when He was near.

In the days of Christ the Jews gave much care to the education of their children. Their schools were connected with the synagogues, or places of worship, and the teachers were called rabbis, men who were supposed to be very learned.

Jesus did not go to these schools, for they taught many things that were not true. Instead of God's Word, the sayings of men were studied, and often these were contrary to that which God had taught through His prophets.

God Himself by His Holy Spirit instructed Mary how to bring up His Son. Mary taught Jesus from the Holy Scriptures, and He learned to read and study them for Himself.

Jesus also loved to study the wonderful things which God had made, in the earth and in the sky. In this book of nature He saw the trees and plants and animals, and the sun and the stars.

Day by day He watched them, and tried to learn lessons from them, and to understand the reason of things.

Holy angels were with Him, and helped Him to learn from these things about God. Thus, as He grew in height and strength, He grew also in knowledge and wisdom.

Every child may gain knowledge as Jesus did. We

should spend our time in learning only that which is true. Falsehood and fables will do us no good.

Only the truth is of any value, and this we may learn from God's Word and from His works. As we study these things the angels will help us to understand.

We shall see the wisdom and goodness of our heavenly Father. Our minds will be strengthened, our hearts will be made pure, and we shall be more like Christ.

Every year Joseph and Mary went up to Jerusalem, to the feast of the Passover. When Jesus was twelve years old, they took Him with them.

This was a pleasant journey. The people traveled on foot, or rode on oxen or asses, and it took several days to go. The distance from Nazareth to Jerusalem is about seventy miles. From all parts of the land, and even from other countries, the people went to this feast, and those from the same place usually traveled together, in a large company.

The feast was held near the close of March or the beginning of April. This was springtime in Palestine, and the whole land was bright with flowers, and glad with the song of birds.

As they traveled, parents told their children of the wonderful things that God had done for Israel in ages past. And often they sang together some of the beautiful psalms of David.

In the days of Christ the people had grown cold and formal in their service to God. They thought more of their own pleasure than of His goodness to them.

But it was not so with Jesus. He loved to think about God. As He came to the temple, He watched the priests in their work. He bowed with the worshipers as they knelt to pray, and His voice joined in the songs of praise.

Every morning and evening a lamb was offered upon the altar. This was to represent the death of the Saviour. As the child Jesus looked upon the innocent victim, the Holy Spirit taught Him its meaning. He knew that He Himself, as the Lamb of God, must die for the sins of men.

With such thoughts in His mind, Jesus wanted to be alone. So He did not stay with His parents in the temple, and when they started for home He was not with them.

In a room connected with the temple there was a school taught by the rabbis, and to this place after a while the child Jesus came. He sat with the other youth at the feet of the great teachers, and listened to their words.

The Jews had many wrong ideas about the Messiah. Jesus knew this, but He did not contradict the learned men. As one who wished to be taught, He asked questions about what the prophets had written.

The fifty-third chapter of Isaiah speaks of the Saviour's death, and Jesus read this chapter, and asked its meaning.

The rabbis could give no answer. They began to question Jesus, and they were astonished at His knowledge of the Scriptures.

They saw that He understood the Bible far better than they did. They saw that their teaching was wrong, but they were not willing to believe anything different.

Yet Jesus was so modest and gentle that they were not angry with Him. They wanted to keep Him as a student, and teach Him to explain the Bible as they did.

When Joseph and Mary left Jerusalem on their journey

toward home, they did not notice that Jesus stayed behind. They thought that He was with some of their friends in the company.

But on stopping to camp for the night, they missed His helpful hand. They looked for Him throughout the company, but in vain.

Joseph and Mary were in great fear. They remembered how Herod had tried to kill Jesus in His infancy, and they were afraid that some evil had now befallen Him.

With sorrowful hearts they hastened back to Jerusalem; but it was not till the third day that they found Him.

Great was their joy at seeing Him again, yet Mary thought that He was to blame for leaving them. She said:

"Son, why hast Thou thus dealt with us? Behold, Thy father and I have sought Thee sorrowing."

"How is it that ye sought Me?" Jesus answered. "Wist ye not that I must be about My Father's business?" Luke 2:48, 49.

As He spoke these words, Jesus pointed upward. On His face was a light at which they wondered. Jesus knew that He was the Son of God, and He had been doing the work for which His Father had sent Him into the world.

Mary never forgot these words. In the years that followed, she better understood their wonderful meaning.

Joseph and Mary loved Jesus, yet they had been careless in losing Him. They had forgotten the very work which God had given them to do. By one day's neglect they lost Jesus.

In the same way today many lose the Saviour from their company. When we do not love to think about Him, or pray to Him; when we speak idle, unkind, or evil words,

3

we separate ourselves from Christ. Without Him, we are lonely and sad.

But if we really desire His company, He will always be with us. With all who seek His presence, the Saviour loves to stay. He will brighten the poorest home, and gladden the lowliest heart.

Though He knew that He was the Son of God, Jesus went home to Nazareth with Joseph and Mary. Until thirty years of age He was "subject unto them." Luke 2:51.

He who had been the Commander of Heaven was on earth a loving and obedient son. The great things brought to His mind by the service of the temple were hidden in His heart. He waited until God's time to begin His appointed work.

Jesus lived in the home of a peasant, a poor man. Faithfully and cheerfully He did His part in helping to support the family. As soon as He was old enough, He learned a trade, and worked in the carpenter's shop with Joseph.

In the coarse dress of a common laborer He passed through the streets of the little town, going to and from His work. He did not use His divine power to make His life easier for Himself.

As Jesus worked in childhood and youth, He grew strong in body and mind. He tried to use all His powers in such a way as to keep them in health, that He might do the best work in every line.

Whatever He did was done well. He wanted to be perfect, even in the handling of tools. By His example He taught that we ought to be industrious, that we should do our work carefully and well, and that such work is honorable. All should find something to do that will be helpful to themselves and to others.

God gave us work as a blessing, and He is pleased with children who cheerfully take their part in the duties of the household, sharing the burdens of father and mother. Such children will go out from the home to be a blessing to others.

The youth who try to please God in all that they do, who do right because it is right, will be useful in the world. By being faithful in a humble place they are fitting themselves for a higher position.

H. HOFMANN

As the learned doctors in Jerusalem listened to the youthful Jesus explain the meaning of God's Word, they were deeply impressed that here was no ordinary lad.

Days of Conflict

THE Jewish teachers made many rules for the people, and required them to do many things that God had not commanded. Even the children had to learn and obey these rules. But Jesus did not try to learn what the rabbis taught. He was careful not to speak disrespectfully of these teachers, but He studied the Scriptures, and obeyed the laws of God.

Often He was reproved for not obeying what others did. Then He showed from the Bible what was the right way.

Jesus was always trying to make others happy. Because He was so kind and gentle, the rabbis hoped to make Him do as they did. But they could not. When urged to obey their rules He asked what the Bible taught. Whatever that said, He would do.

This made the rabbis angry. They knew that their rules were contrary to the Bible, and yet they were displeased with Jesus for refusing to obey them.

They complained of Him to His parents. Joseph and

37

Mary thought the rabbis good men, and Jesus suffered blame, which was hard to bear.

The brothers of Jesus took sides with the rabbis. The words of these teachers, they said, should be heeded as the word of God. They reproved Jesus for setting Himself above the leaders of the people.

The rabbis thought themselves better than other men, and they would not associate with the common people. The poor and ignorant they despised. Even the sick and suffering they left without hope or comfort.

Jesus showed a loving interest in all men. Every suffering one whom He met, He tried to help. He had little money to give, but He often denied Himself of food in order to help others.

When His brothers spoke harshly to poor, wretched beings, Jesus would go to these very ones and speak words of kindness and encouragement.

To those who were hungry and thirsty, He would bring a cup of cold water, and often would give them the food intended for His own meal.

All this displeased His brothers. They threatened and tried to terrify Him, but He kept right on, doing as God had said.

Many were the trials and temptations that Jesus had to meet. Satan was always watching to overcome Him.

If Jesus could have been led to do one wrong act, or to speak one impatient word, He could not have been our Saviour, and the whole world would have been lost. Satan knew this, and it was for this reason that he tried so hard to lead Jesus into sin.

The Saviour was always guarded by heavenly angels,

yet His life was one long struggle against the powers of darkness. Not one of us will ever have to meet such fierce temptations as He did.

But to every temptation He had one answer: "It is written." The wrongdoing of His brothers He did not often rebuke, but He told them what God had said.

Nazareth was a wicked town, and the children and youth tried to have Jesus follow their evil ways. He was bright and cheerful, and they liked His company.

But His godly principles roused their anger. Often for refusing to join in some forbidden act, He was called a coward. Often He was sneered at, as being altogether too particular about little things. To all this His answer was: "It is written." "The fear of the Lord, that is wisdom; and to depart from evil is understanding." Job 28:28. To love evil is to love death, for "the wages of sin is death." Romans 6:23.

Jesus did not contend for His rights. When roughly used, He bore it patiently. Because He was so willing and uncomplaining, His work was often made needlessly hard. Yet He was not discouraged for He knew that God smiled upon Him.

His happiest hours were found when alone with nature and with God. When His work was done, He loved to go into the fields, to meditate in the green valleys, to pray to God on the mountainside, or amid the trees of the forest.

He listened to the lark caroling forth music to its Creator, and His voice joined the song of joyful praise and thanksgiving.

With the voice of singing He welcomed the morning light. The break of day often found Him in some quiet place, thinking about God, studying the Bible, or in prayer.

From these peaceful hours He would return to His home to take up His duties again, and to give an example of patient toil. Wherever He was, His presence seemed to bring the angels near. The influence of His pure, holy life was felt by all classes of people.

Harmless and undefiled, He walked among the thoughtless, the rude, the uncourteous; amid the unjust taxgatherers, the reckless prodigals, the unrighteous Samaritans, the heathen soldiers, and the rough peasants.

He spoke a word of sympathy here, and a word there, as He saw men weary, yet compelled to bear heavy burdens. He shared their burdens, and repeated to them the lessons He had learned from nature, of the love, the kindness, the goodness of God.

He taught them to look upon themselves as having precious talents, which if rightly used would gain for them eternal riches. By His own example He taught that every moment of time is of value, and should be put to some good use.

He passed by no human being as worthless, but tried to encourage the roughest and most unpromising. He told them that God loved them as His children, and that they might become like Him in character.

So in a quiet way Jesus from His very childhood worked for others. This work none of the learned teachers, nor even His own brothers, could make Him give up. With an earnest purpose He carried out the design of His life, for He was to be the light of the world.

"This Is My Beloved Son"

The baptism of Jesus was not performed by John
because of any need Jesus had for cleansing from
sin, but to give us an example that we should do
as He had done.

PAINTING BY C. L. WOODWARD

The Baptism

WHEN the time for Christ's public ministry had come, His first act was to go to the river Jordan, and be baptized by John the Baptist.

John had been sent to prepare the way for the Saviour. He had preached in the wilderness, saying:

"The kingdom of God is at hand: repent ye, and believe the gospel." Mark 1:15.

Multitudes flocked to hear him. Many were convicted of their sins, and were baptized by him in the Jordan.

God had made known to John that some day the Messiah would come to him and ask to be baptized. He had also promised that a sign should be given him, so that he might know who it was.

When Jesus came, John saw in His face such signs of His holy life, that he forbade Him, saying: "I have need to be baptized of Thee, and comest Thou to me?

"And Jesus answering said unto him, Suffer it to be so now: for thus it becometh us to fulfil all righteousness." Matthew 3:14, 15.

41

And as He said this, there was seen upon His face the same heavenly light that Simeon had beheld.

So John led the Saviour down into the waters of the beautiful Jordan, and there he baptized Him in the sight of all the people.

Jesus was not baptized to show repentance for His own sins; for He had never sinned. He did it to set an example for us.

When He came up out of the water, He kneeled on the riverbank, and prayed. Then the heavens were opened, beams of glory streamed forth, "and He saw the Spirit of God descending like a dove, and lighting upon Him." Matthew 3:16.

His face and form were all aglow with the light of the glory of God. And from Heaven the voice of God was heard saying:

"This is My beloved Son, in whom I am well pleased." Matthew 3:16, 17.

The glory that rested upon Christ was a pledge of the love of God for us. The Saviour came as our example; and just as surely as God heard His prayer, He will hear ours.

The most needy, the most sinful, the most despised, may find access to the Father. When we come to Him in Jesus' name, the voice which spoke to Jesus speaks to us, saying: "This is My beloved child, in whom I am well pleased."

The Temptation

*A*FTER His baptism, Christ was led by the Spirit into the wilderness, to be tempted of the devil.

In going into the wilderness, Christ was led by the Spirit of God. He did not invite temptation. He wanted to be alone, that he might contemplate His mission and work.

By prayer and fasting He was to brace Himself for the bloodstained path He must travel. But Satan knew where the Saviour had gone; so he went there to tempt Him.

As Christ left the Jordan, His face was lighted with the glory of God. But after He entered the wilderness, this glory disappeared.

The sins of the world were upon Him, and His face showed such sorrow and anguish as man had never felt. He was suffering for sinners.

Adam and Eve in Eden had disobeyed God by eating of the forbidden fruit. Their disobedience had brought sin and sorrow and death into the world.

Christ came to give an example of obedience. In the

CARL BLOCH

Jesus won a mighty victory over Satan when faced with three great temptations,
and His weapon was one we all can use—God's Word.

wilderness, after fasting forty days, He would not, even to obtain food, depart from the will of His Father.

One of the temptations that overcame our first parents was the temptation to indulge appetite. By this long fast Christ was to show that appetite can be brought under control.

Satan tempts men to indulgence, because this weakens the body and beclouds the mind. Then he knows that he can the more easily deceive and destroy them.

But Christ's example teaches that every wrong desire must be overcome. Our appetites are not to rule us; we must rule them.

When Satan first appeared to Christ, he looked like an angel of light. He claimed to be a messenger from Heaven.

He told Jesus that it was not the will of His Father that He should endure this suffering; He was to show only a willingness to suffer.

When Jesus was struggling against the keenest pangs of hunger, Satan said to Him:

"If Thou be the Son of God, command that these stones be made bread."

But since the Saviour had come to live as our example, He must endure suffering as we have to endure it; He must not work a miracle for His own good. His miracles were all to be for the good of others. To the demand of Satan He answered:

"It is written, Man shall not live by bread alone, but by every word that proceedeth out of the mouth of God."

Thus He showed that it is far less important to provide ourselves with food than that we should obey the word of God. Those who obey God's word have the promise of all things needed for the present life, and they have also the promise of future life.

Satan had failed to overcome Christ in the first great temptation; he next carried Him to a pinnacle of the temple at Jerusalem, and said:

"If thou be the Son of God, cast Thyself down: for it is written, He shall give His angels charge concerning Thee: and in their hands they shall bear Thee up, lest at any time Thou dash Thy foot against a stone."

Satan here followed Christ's example in quoting Scripture. But this promise is not for those who willfully venture into danger. God had not told Jesus to throw Himself down from the temple. Jesus would not do it to please Satan. He said: "It is written again, Thou shalt not tempt the Lord thy God."

We should trust in the care of our heavenly Father; but we must not go where He does not send us. We must not do what He has forbidden.

Because God is merciful, and ready to forgive, there are those who say that it is safe to disobey Him. But this is presumption. God will forgive all who seek pardon and turn away from sin. But those who choose to disobey Him He can not bless.

Satan now appeared what he really was—the prince of the powers of darkness. He took Jesus to the top of a high mountain, and showed Him all the kingdoms of the world.

The sunlight lay on splendid cities, marble palaces, fruitful fields, and vineyards. Satan said:

"All these things will I give Thee, if Thou wilt fall down and worship me."

For a moment Christ looked upon the scene. Then He turned away. Satan had presented the world to Him in the most attractive light; but the Saviour looked beneath the outward beauty.

He saw the world in its wretchedness and sin, apart from God. All this misery was the result of man's turning away from God to worship Satan.

Christ was filled with longing to redeem that which was lost. He longed to restore the world to more than its Eden beauty. He wanted to place men on vantage ground with God.

For sinful man He was withstanding temptation. He was to be an overcomer, that they might overcome, that they might be equal with the angels, and be worthy to be acknowledged as sons of God.

To Satan's demand for worship, Christ answered:

"Get thee hence, Satan: for it is written, Thou shalt worship the Lord thy God, and Him only shalt thou serve." Matthew 4:3-10.

The love of the world, the lust for power, and the pride of life—everything that draws man away from the worship of God—was embraced in this great temptation of Christ.

Satan offered Christ the world and its riches if He would pay homage to the principles of evil. So Satan presents to us the advantages to be gained by wrongdoing.

He whispers to us, "In order to succeed in this world, you must serve me. Do not be too particular about truth and honesty. Obey my counsel, and I will give you riches, honor, and happiness."

In obeying this counsel we are worshiping Satan instead of God. It will bring us only misery and ruin.

Christ has shown us what we should do when tempted.

When He said to Satan, "Get thee hence," the tempter could not resist the command. He was compelled to go.

Writhing with baffled hate and rage, the rebel chief left the presence of the world's Redeemer.

The contest was ended for the time. Christ's victory was as complete as had been the failure of Adam.

So we may resist temptation, and overcome Satan. The Lord says to us, "Resist the devil, and he will flee from you. Draw nigh to God, and He will draw nigh to you." James 4:7, 8.

Early Ministry

*F*ROM the wilderness, Christ returned to the Jordan, where John the Baptist was preaching. At that time men sent by the rulers at Jerusalem were questioning John as to his authority for teaching and baptizing the people.

They asked if he was the Messiah, or Elijah, or "that prophet," meaning Moses. To all this he answered, "I am not." Then they asked: "Who art thou? that we may give an answer to them that sent us.

"He said, I am the voice of one crying in the wilderness, Make straight the way of the Lord, as said the prophet Esaias." John 1:22, 23.

In old times when a king had to travel from one part of his country to another, men were sent ahead of his chariot to prepare the roads.

They had to cut down trees, gather out the stones, and fill up the hollows, so that the way would be clear for the king.

So when Jesus, the heavenly King, was coming, John the

Baptist was sent to prepare the way by telling the people, and calling on them to repent of their sins.

As John answered the messengers from Jerusalem, he saw Jesus standing on the riverbank. His face lighted up, and stretching out his hands, he said:

"There standeth One among you, whom ye know not; He it is, who coming after me is preferred before me, whose shoe's latchet I am not worthy to unloose." John 1:26, 27.

The people were greatly moved. The Messiah was among them! They looked about eagerly to find the One of whom John had spoken. But Jesus had mingled with the multitude, and was lost to sight.

The next day John again saw Jesus, and, pointing to Him, cried: "Behold the Lamb of God, which taketh away the sin of the world!"

Then John told of the sign that had been seen at Christ's baptism. "I saw, and bare record," he added, "that this is the Son of God." John 1:29, 34.

With awe and wonder the hearers looked upon Jesus. They questioned with themselves, Is this the Christ?

They saw that Jesus bore no tokens of worldly wealth or greatness. His clothing was plain and simple, such as poor people wore. But in His pale, worn face was something that moved their hearts.

In that face they read dignity and power; and every glance of the eye, every feature of the countenance, spoke of divine compassion and unutterable love.

But the messengers from Jerusalem were not drawn to the Saviour. John had not said that which they desired to hear. They expected the Messiah to come as a great conqueror. They saw that this was not the mission of Jesus, and in disappointment they turned from Him.

The next day John again saw Jesus, and again he cried, "Behold the Lamb of God!" John 1:36. Two of John's disciples were standing near, and they followed Jesus. They listened to His teaching, and became His disciples. One of the two was Andrew, the other John.

Andrew soon brought to Jesus his own brother, Simon, whom Christ named Peter. The next day, on the way to Galilee, Christ called another disciple, Philip. As soon as Philip found the Saviour, he brought his friend Nathaniel.

In this way Christ's great work on earth was begun. One by one He called His disciples, and one brought his brother, another his friend. This is what every follower of Christ is to do. As soon as he himself knows Jesus, he is to tell others what a precious Friend he has found. This is a work that all can do, whether they are young or old.

At Cana in Galilee, Christ, with his disciples, attended a marriage feast. For the happiness of this household gathering, His wonderful power was put forth.

It was the custom in that country to use wine on such occasions. Before the feast was ended, the supply of wine had failed. The lack of wine at a feast would be thought to show a want of hospitality, and this was regarded as a great disgrace.

Christ was told of what had happened, and He bade the servants fill six large stone jars with water. Then He said, "Draw out now, and bear unto the governor of the feast." John 2:8.

Instead of water, there came forth wine. This wine was

CARL BLOCH

The first miracle Jesus performed was that of turning water into wine at a marriage feast. This showed His approval of such gatherings and His courtesy in assisting His host and guests at a time of need.

much better than that which had been served before, and there was enough for all.

After working the miracle, Jesus quietly went away. Not till He had gone, did the guests know of the work He had done.

Christ's gift to the marriage feast was a symbol. The water represented baptism, and the wine His blood, that was to be shed for the world.

The wine which Jesus made was not fermented liquor. Such wine is a cause of drunkenness and many great evils, and God had forbidden its use. He says, "Wine is a mocker, strong drink is raging: and whosoever is deceived thereby is not wise." "It biteth like a serpent, and stingeth like an adder." Proverbs 20:1; 23:32.

The wine used at the feast was the pure, sweet juice of the grape. It was like that which the prophet Isaiah calls "the new wine . . . in the cluster;" and he says, "A blessing is in it." Isaiah 65:8.

By going to the marriage feast, Christ showed that it is right to meet together in this pleasant way. He liked to see people happy. Often He visited them in their homes, and tried to have them forget their cares and their troubles, and think of God's goodness and His love. Wherever He might be, Christ was always trying to do this. Wherever a heart was open to receive the divine message, He unfolded the truths of the way of salvation.

One day, as He was passing through the country of Samaria, He sat down by a well to rest. When a woman came to draw water, He asked her for a drink.

The woman wondered at this, for she knew how the Jews hated the Samaritans. But Christ told her that if she

ELSIE ANNA WOOD

The love of Jesus for all lost humanity and His desire to save them were shown in His conversation with the Samaritan woman at the well. She responded to the gracious words and found salvation for herself and many others with her.

would ask of Him, He would give her living water. At this she wondered the more. Then Jesus said to her:

"Whosoever drinketh of this water shall thirst again: but whosoever drinketh of the water that I shall give him shall never thirst; but the water that I shall give him shall be in him a well of water springing up into everlasting life." John 4:13, 14. By the living water is meant the Holy Spirit. As a thirsty traveler needs water to drink, so do we need God's Spirit in our hearts. He who drinks of this water shall never thirst.

The Holy Spirit brings God's love into our hearts. It satisfies our longings, so that the riches and honors and pleasures of this world do not attract us. And it fills us with such joy that we want others to have it too. It will be in us like a spring of water, that flows out in blessing to all around.

And every one in whom God's Spirit dwells, will live forever with Christ in His kingdom. Received into the heart by faith, it is the beginning of the life eternal.

This precious blessing Christ told the woman He would give her if she asked for it. So He will give it to us.

This woman had broken God's commandments, and Christ showed her that He knew the sins of her life. But He showed, too, that He was her friend, that He loved and pitied her, and that if she was willing to forsake her sins, God would receive her as His child.

How glad she was to know this! In her joy she hurried away to the town near by, and called the people to come and see Jesus.

So they came to the well, and asked Him to stay with them. He remained two days, and taught them, and many listened to His words. They repented of their sins, and believed on Him as their Saviour.

During His ministry, Jesus twice visited His old home at Nazareth. At the first visit He went to the synagogue on the Sabbath day.

Here He read from Isaiah's prophecy about the work of the Messiah—how He was to preach good tidings to the poor, to comfort the sorrowing, to give sight to the blind, and to heal those that were bruised.

Then He told the people that all this was fulfilled that day. This was the work that He Himself was doing.

At these words the hearers were filled with joy. They believed that Jesus was the promised Saviour. Their hearts were moved upon by the Holy Spirit, and they responded with fervent amens and praises to the Lord.

Then they remembered how Jesus had lived among them as a carpenter. Often they had seen Him working in the shop with Joseph. Though in His whole life there had been only deeds of love and mercy, they would not believe that He was the Messiah.

By such thoughts as these they opened the way for Satan to control their minds. Then they were filled with wrath against the Saviour. They cried out against Him, and determined to take His life.

They hurried Him away, meaning to throw Him over the steep side of a hill. But holy angels were near to protect Him. He passed safely through the crowd, and was not to be found.

The next time He came to Nazareth, the people were no more ready to receive Him. He went away, never to return.

Christ worked for those who wanted His help, and all through the country the people flocked about Him. As He healed and taught them, there was great rejoicing. Heaven seemed to come down to the earth, and they feasted upon the grace of a merciful Saviour.

CARL BLOCH

Never man spake as Jesus spake. In His beautiful Sermon on the Mount, He explained what God thinks most precious and what would give real joy and happiness to every heart.

Teachings of Christ

*A*MONG the Jews, religion had come to be little more than a round of ceremonies. As they had departed from the true worship of God, and lost the spiritual power of His word, they had tried to supply the lack by adding ceremonies and traditions of their own.

Only the blood of Christ can cleanse from sin. Only His power can keep men from sinning. But the Jews depended upon their own works and ceremonies of their religion to earn for them salvation. Because of their zeal for these ceremonies they thought themselves righteous, and worthy of a place in God's kingdom.

But their hopes were fixed on worldly greatness. They longed for riches and power, and these they expected as the reward for their pretended piety.

They looked for the Messiah to set up His kingdom on this earth, and to rule as a mighty prince among men. Every worldly blessing they hoped to receive at His coming.

Jesus knew that their hopes were to be disappointed. He had come to teach them of something far better than they had sought.

He had come to restore the true worship of God. He was to bring in a pure heart religion, that would manifest itself in a pure life and a holy character.

In the beautiful Sermon on the Mount He explained what God thinks most precious, and what would give real happiness.

The Saviour's disciples had been influenced by the teachings of the rabbis; and for these disciples, first of all, Christ's lessons were spoken. That which He taught them is for us also. We need to learn the same things.

"Blessed are the poor in spirit," Christ said. Matthew 5:3. The poor in spirit are those who know their own sinfulness and need. They know that of themselves they can do no good thing. They desire help from God, and to them His blessing is given.

"For thus saith the high and lofty One that inhabiteth eternity, whose name is Holy; I dwell in the high and holy place, with him also that is of a contrite and humble spirit, to revive the spirit of the humble, and to revive the heart of the contrite ones." Isaiah 57:15.

"Blessed are they that mourn." Matthew 5:4. This does not mean those who complain and murmur, and who go about with a sour, downcast look. It means those who are truly sorry for their sins, and who ask God for pardon.

All such He will freely forgive. He says, "I will turn their mourning into joy, and will comfort them, and make them rejoice from their sorrow." Jeremiah 31:13.

"Blessed are the meek." Matthew 5:5. Christ says, "Learn of Me; for I am meek and lowly in heart." Matthew 11:29. When He was wrongfully treated, He returned good for evil. In this He has given us an example, that we should do as He has done.

"Blessed are they which do hunger and thirst after righteousness." Righteousness is right-doing. It is obedience to the law of God; for in that law the principles of righteousness are set forth. The Bible says, "All Thy commandments are righteousness." Psalm 119:172.

That law Christ, by His example, taught men to obey. The righteousness of the law is seen in His life. We hunger and thirst after righteousness when we want to have all our thoughts, our words, and our actions, like Christ's.

And we may be like Christ if we really desire to be. We may have our lives like His life, our actions in harmony with the law of God. The Holy Spirit will bring God's love into our hearts, so that we shall delight to do His will.

God is more willing to give us His Spirit than parents are to give good things to their children. His promise is, "Ask, and it shall be given you." Luke 11:9; Matthew 7:7. All that hunger and thirst after righteousness "shall be filled."

"Blessed are the merciful." Matthew 5:7. To be merciful is to treat others better than they deserve. So God has treated us. He delights to show mercy. He is kind to the unthankful and to the evil.

So He teaches us to treat one another. He says, "Be ye kind one to another, tenderhearted, forgiving one another, even as God for Christ's sake hath forgiven you." Ephesians 4:32.

"Blessed are the pure in heart." Matthew 5:8. God cares more for what we really are than for what we say we are. He does not care how beautiful we may look, but He

wants our hearts pure. Then all our words and actions will
be right.

King David prayed, "Create in me a clean heart, O God."
"Let the words of my mouth, and the meditation of my
heart, be acceptable in Thy sight, O Lord, my strength, and
my Redeemer." Psalm 51:10; 19:14. This should be our
prayer.

"Blessed are the peacemakers." Matthew 5:9. He who
has the meek and lowly spirit of Christ will be a peacemaker.
Such a spirit provokes no quarrel, gives back no angry
answer. It makes the home happy, and brings a sweet peace
that blesses all around.

"Blessed are they which are persecuted for righteousness' sake." Matthew 5:10. Christ knew that for His sake
many of His disciples would be put in prison, and many
would be killed. But He told them not to mourn because
of this.

Nothing can harm those who love and follow Christ.
He will be with them in every place. They may be put to
death, but He will give them a life that will never end, and
a crown of glory that fadeth not away.

And from them others will learn about the dear Saviour.
Christ said to His disciples:

"Ye are the light of the world." Matthew 5:14. Jesus
was soon going away from the world to His heavenly
home. But the disciples were to teach the people of His
love. They were to be as lights among men.

The lamp in the lighthouse, shining out in the darkness,
guides the ship safely to the harbor; thus Christ's followers are to shine in this dark world, to guide men to Christ and
the heavenly home.

This is what all the followers of Christ are to do. He calls them to work with Him in saving others.

Such lessons were strange and new to Christ's hearers, and He repeated them many times. At one time a lawyer came to Him with the question: "Master, what shall I do to inherit eternal life?" Jesus said unto him, "What is written in the law? how readest thou?

"And he answering said, Thou shalt love the Lord thy God with all thy heart, and with all thy soul, and with all thy strength, and with all thy mind; and thy neighbor as thyself.

"Thou hast answered right," said Christ; "this do and thou shalt live." The lawyer had not done this. He knew that he had not loved others as himself. Instead of repenting, he tried to find an excuse for his selfishness. So he asked Jesus: "Who is my neighbor?" Luke 10:25-29.

The priests and rabbis often disputed about this question. They did not call the poor and ignorant their neighbors, and would show them no kindness. Christ took no part in their disputes; He answered the question by a story about something that had happened a short time before.

A certain man, He said, was going down from Jerusalem to Jericho. The road was steep and rocky, and passed through a wild, lonely region. Here the man was seized by robbers, and stripped of all that he had. He was beaten and bruised, and left for dead.

As he lay thus, a priest and then a Levite from the temple at Jerusalem came that way. But instead of helping the poor man, they passed by on the other side.

ELSIE ANNA WOOD

The story which Jesus told of the good Samaritan who came to the aid of a fellow man in distress, should help us understand that all men are our neighbors, and that we show our love to God by being kind to them.

These men had been chosen to minister in God's temple, and they ought to have been like Him, full of mercy and kindness. But their hearts were cold and unfeeling.

After a time a Samaritan came near. The Samaritans were despised and hated by the Jews. To one of these people a Jew would not give so much as a drink of water or a morsel of bread. But the Samaritan did not stop to think of this. He did not stop even to think of the robbers who might be watching for him.

There lay the stranger, bleeding and ready to die. The Samaritan took off his own cloak, and wrapped it about him.

He gave him his own wine to drink, and poured oil on his wounds. He put him on his own beast, brought him to an inn, and took care of him all night.

The next morning, before going away, he paid the inn-keeper to care for him till he should be strong again. So Jesus told the story. Then turning to the lawyer, He asked:

"Which now of these three, thinkest thou, was neighbor unto him that fell among the thieves?"

The lawyer answered, "He that showed mercy on him."

Then Jesus said, "Go, and do thou likewise." Luke 10:35-37. So Jesus taught that every person who needs our help is our neighbor. We are to treat him just as we ourselves would like to be treated.

The priest and the Levite pretended to keep God's commandments, but it was the Samaritan who really kept them. His heart was kind and loving.

In taking care of the wounded stranger, he was showing love to God as well as to man. For it pleases God to have

5

us do good to one another. We show our love for Him by being kind to those about us.

A kind, loving heart is worth more than all the riches in the world. Those who live to do good show that they are children of God. They are the ones who will dwell with Christ in His kingdom.

Sabbathkeeping

*T*HE SAVIOUR kept the Sabbath, and taught His disciples to keep it. He knew how it should be kept, for He Himself had made it holy.

The Bible says, "Remember the Sabbath day, to keep it holy." "The seventh day is the Sabbath of the Lord thy God." "For in six days the Lord made heaven and earth, the sea, and all that in them is, and rested the seventh day: wherefore the Lord blessed the Sabbath day, and hallowed it." Exodus 20: 8, 10, 11; 31: 16, 17. Christ had worked with His Father in creating the earth, and He had made the Sabbath. The Bible says that "all things were made by Him." John 1: 3.

When we look on the sun and the stars, the trees and the beautiful flowers, we should remember that Christ made them all. And He made the Sabbath to help us keep in mind His love and power.

The Jewish teachers had made many rules about the way to keep the Sabbath, and they wanted every one to obey their rules. So they watched the Saviour, to see what He would do.

Jesus defended His disciples when they picked some grain on the Sabbath to satisfy their hunger, and thus He showed that the Sabbath was to be a blessing and not a burden.

One Sabbath, as Christ and His disciples were going home from the synagogue, they passed through a field of grain. It was late, and the disciples were hungry. So they broke off some of the heads of grain, rubbed them in their hands, and ate the kernels.

On any other day, one passing through a field or an orchard was allowed to gather what he wanted to eat. But it was not so on the Sabbath. Christ's enemies saw what the disciples were doing, and they said to the Saviour:

"Behold, Thy disciples do that which is not lawful to do upon the Sabbath day." Matthew 12: 2.

But Christ defended His followers. He reminded His accusers of David, who, when in need, had eaten of the sacred bread of the tabernacle, and had given it to his hungry followers.

If it was right for David when hungry to eat this sacred bread, then was it not right for the disciples when hungry to pluck the grain on the sacred hours of the Sabbath?

The Sabbath was not made to be a burden to man. It was to do him good, to give him peace and rest. Therefore our Lord said, "The Sabbath was made for man, and not man for the Sabbath." Mark 2: 27.

"And it came to pass also on another Sabbath, that He entered into the synagogue and taught: and there was a man whose right hand was withered.

"And the scribes and Pharisees watched Him, whether He would heal on the Sabbath day; that they might find an accusation against Him.

"But He knew their thoughts, and said to the man which had the withered hand, Rise up, and stand forth in the midst. And he arose and stood forth.

"Then said Jesus unto them, I will ask you one thing; Is it lawful on the Sabbath days to do good, or to do evil? to save life, or to destroy it?"

"And when He had looked round about on them with anger, being grieved for the hardness of their hearts, He saith unto the man, Stretch forth thine hand. And he stretched it out: and his hand was restored whole as the other."

"And they were filled with madness; and communed one with another what they might do to Jesus." Luke 6:6-9, 11; Mark 3:5.

The Saviour showed how unreasonable they were, by asking them a question. "And He said unto them, What man shall there be among you, that shall have one sheep, and if it fall into a pit on the Sabbath day, will he not lay hold on it, and lift it out?"

This they could not answer. So He said, "How much then is a man better than a sheep? Wherefore it is lawful to do well on the Sabbath days." Matthew 12:11, 12.

"It is lawful;" that is, it is according to law. Christ never reproved the Jews for keeping the law of God, or for honoring the Sabbath. On the contrary, He ever upheld the law in all its completeness.

Isaiah prophesied of Christ, "He will magnify the law, and make it honorable." Isaiah 42:21. To magnify is to make larger, to raise to a higher position.

Christ magnified the law by showing in every part its wonderful meaning. He showed that it is to be obeyed, not only in the actions, which are seen by men, but in the thoughts, which are known only to God.

To those who claimed that He came to set aside the law,

He said, "Think not that I am come to destroy the law, or the prophets: I am not come to destroy, but to fulfil." Matthew 5:17.

To fulfill means to keep, or perform. (James 2:8.) So when He came to be baptized by John the Baptist, He said, "Thus it becometh us to fulfil all righteousness." Matthew 3:15. To fulfill the law is to obey it perfectly.

God's law can never be changed; for Christ said, "Till heaven and earth pass, one jot or one tittle shall in no wise pass from the law, till all be fulfilled." Matthew 5:18.

When He asked the question, "Is it lawful on the Sabbath days to do good, or to do evil? to save life, or to destroy it?" Christ showed that He could read the hearts of the wicked Pharisees who accused Him.

While He was trying to save life by healing the sick, they were trying to destroy life by putting Him to death. Was it better to slay upon the Sabbath, as they were planning to do, than to cure the suffering ones, as He had done?

Was it better to have murder in the heart on God's holy day than to have love toward all men—love which is shown in kindness and deeds of mercy?

Many times the Jews charged Christ with breaking the Sabbath. Often they tried to kill Him because He did not keep it according to their traditions. But this made no difference with Him. He kept the Sabbath as God wanted it to be kept.

In Jerusalem there was a large pool of water called Bethesda. At certain times this pool was troubled; the people believed that an angel of the Lord went down into it, and stirred the waters, and that the first one who stepped in after the waters were stirred would be cured of whatever disease he had.

Great numbers of people came to the place, hoping to be cured; but most of them were disappointed. At the moving of the waters there was such a crowd, that many could not even get to the edge of the pool.

One Sabbath day Jesus came to Bethesda. His heart was filled with pity as He saw the poor sufferers there.

One man seemed more wretched than the others. For thirty-eight years he had been a helpless cripple. No doctor could cure him. Many times he had been brought to Bethesda; but when the waters were troubled, another would step in before him.

On this Sabbath he had tried once more to reach the pool, but in vain. Jesus saw him as he crept back to the mat which was his bed. His strength was almost gone. Unless help should come soon, he must die.

As he lay thus, now and then lifting his eyes to look at the pool, a loving face bent over him, and he heard a voice say, "Wilt thou be made whole?"

The man answered sorrowfully, "Sir, I have no man, when the water is troubled, to put me into the pool: but while I am coming, another steppeth down before me."

He did not know that the One beside him could heal, not one only, but all who should come to Him. Christ said to the man: "Rise, take up thy bed, and walk."

At once he tried to obey the command, and strength came to him. He sprang to his feet, and found that he could stand and could walk. What a delight it was!

He took up his bed and hurried away, praising God at every step. Soon he met some of the Pharisees, and told them of his wonderful cure. They did not seem glad, but reproved him for carrying his bed on the Sabbath day. The man told them, "He that made me whole, the same said unto me, Take up thy bed, and walk." John 5:1-11.

Then they were no longer displeased with him, but they blamed the one who had told him to carry his bed on the Sabbath day.

At Jerusalem, where the Saviour now was, many of the learned rabbis lived. Here their false ideas about the Sabbath were taught to the people. Great numbers came to worship at the temple, and thus the rabbis' teaching was spread far and wide. Christ wished to correct these errors. This was why He healed the man on the Sabbath day, and told him to carry his bed. He knew that this act would attract the attention of the rabbis, and thus would give Him an opportunity to instruct them. So it proved. The Pharisees brought Christ before the Sanhedrin, the chief council of the Jews, to answer the charge of Sabbathbreaking.

The Saviour declared that His action was in harmony with the Sabbath law. It was in harmony with the will and the work of God. "My Father worketh hitherto," He said, "and I work." John 5:17.

God works continually in sustaining every living thing. Was His work to cease upon the Sabbath day? Should God forbid the sun to fulfill its office on the Sabbath? Should He cut off its rays from warming the earth and nourishing vegetation?

Should the brooks stay from watering the fields, and the waves of the sea still their ebbing and flowing? Must the wheat and maize stop growing, and the trees and flowers put forth no bud or blossom on the Sabbath?

Then man would miss the fruits of the earth, and the blessings that sustain his life. Nature must continue her work, or man would die. And man also has a work to do on this day. The necessities of life must be attended to, the sick must be cared for, the wants of the needy must be supplied. God does not desire His creatures to suffer an hour's pain that may be relieved on the Sabbath or any other day.

Heaven's work never ceases, and we should never rest from doing good. Our own work the law forbids us to do on the rest day of the Lord. The toil for a livelihood must cease; no labor for worldly pleasure or profit is lawful upon that day. But the Sabbath is not to be spent in useless inactivity. As God ceased from His labor of creating, and rested upon the Sabbath, so we are to rest. He bids us lay aside our daily occupations, and devote those sacred hours to healthful rest, to worship, and to holy deeds.

The Good Shepherd

*T*HE SAVIOUR spoke of Himself as a shepherd, and of the disciples as His flock. He said: "I am the Good Shepherd, and know My sheep, and am known of Mine." John 10:14.

Christ was soon to leave His disciples, and He said this to give them comfort. When He should be no more with them, they would remember His words.

Whenever they saw a shepherd watching his flock, they would think of the Saviour's love and care for them.

In that land the shepherd stayed with his flock day and night. Over the rocky hills and through the forests he led them by day, to pleasant, grassy fields by the riverside.

Through the night he watched them, guarding them from wild beasts and from robbers, that were often lurking near.

Tenderly He cared for the feeble and sickly ones. The little lambs He took in His arms, and carried in His bosom.

However large the flock, the shepherd knew every sheep. He had a name for each, and called it by its name.

So Christ, the heavenly Shepherd, cares for His flock

75

that is scattered throughout the world. He knows us all by name. He knows the very house in which we live, and the name of each inmate. He cares for each one as if there were not another in the whole world.

The shepherd went before his sheep, and met all the dangers. He encountered the wild beasts and the robbers. Sometimes the shepherd was killed while guarding his flock.

So the Saviour guards His flock of disciples. He has gone before us. He has lived on earth, as we live. He was a child, a youth, a man. He overcame Satan and all his temptations, so that we may overcome.

He died to save us. Though now He is in Heaven, He does not forget us for a moment. He will safely keep every sheep. Not one that follows Him can be taken by the great enemy.

A shepherd might have a hundred sheep, but if one was missing he did not stay with those that were in the fold. He went to search for the lost one.

Out in the dark night, through the storm, over mountains and valleys, he would go. He would not rest till the sheep was found.

Then he took it in his arms, and carried it back to the fold. He did not complain of the long, hard search, but gladly said:

"Rejoice with me; for I have found my sheep which was lost." Luke 15:4-7.

So the care of the Saviour-Shepherd is not for those only who are in the fold. He says, "The Son of man is come to save that which was lost." Matthew 18:11.

"I say unto you, That likewise joy shall be in heaven over one sinner that repenteth, more than over ninety and nine just persons, which need no repentance." Luke 15:7.

We have sinned, and have wandered away from God. Christ says we are like the sheep that has wandered away from the fold. He came to help us live without sin. This He calls bringing us back to the fold.

When we return with the Shepherd, and cease to sin, Christ says to the angels in Heaven: "Rejoice with Me; for I have found My sheep which was lost."

And a joyful anthem rings out from the angelic choir, filling all Heaven with richest melody.

Christ presents to us no picture of a sorrowful shepherd returning without the sheep. Here is a pledge that not even one of the straying sheep of God's fold is overlooked.

Not one is left unhelped. Every one that will submit to be ransomed, the Saviour will rescue from the wilds of sin.

Then let every wanderer from the fold take courage. The Good Shepherd is searching for you. Remember that His work is "to save that which was lost." That means you.

To doubt the possibility of your salvation is to doubt the saving power of Him who purchased you at an infinite cost. Let faith take the place of unbelief. Look at the hands that were pierced for you, and rejoice in their power to save.

Remember that God and Christ are interested in you, and that all the host of Heaven are engaged in the work for the salvation of sinners.

While Christ was on earth, He showed by His miracles that He had power to save unto the uttermost. By curing the diseases of the body, He showed that He was able to take away sin from the heart.

He caused the lame to walk, the deaf to hear, and the

ELSIE ANNA WOOD

Jesus was kind to Jairus, He raised his little girl from the dead.

blind to see. He cleansed the poor lepers, and healed the man with palsy, and those who had all kinds of diseases.

By His word, even the devils were driven out from the ones whom they had been possessing. Those who saw this wonderful work were astonished, and said: "What a word is this! For with authority and power He commandeth the unclean spirits, and they come out!" Luke 4:36.

At the command of Jesus, Peter was able to walk on the water. But he had to keep his eyes on the Saviour. As soon as he looked away, he began to doubt and sink.

Then he cried, "Lord, save me," and the Saviour's hand was stretched forth to lift him up. Matthew 14:28-31. So whenever one cries to Him for help, the hand of Christ is stretched forth to save.

The Saviour raised the dead to life. One of these was the widow's son at Nain. The people were carrying him to the grave, when they met Jesus. He took the young man by the hand, lifted him up, and gave him alive to his mother. Then the company went back to their homes with shouts of rejoicing and praise to God.

So also the daughter of Jairus was raised, and by Christ's word, Lazarus, who had been dead four days, was called forth from the tomb.

So when Christ shall come to earth again, His voice will pierce the tombs, and "the dead in Christ shall rise" to glorious, immortal life; and so shall they "ever be with the Lord." 1 Thessalonians 4:16, 17.

It was a wonderful work done by our Lord during His ministry on earth. Of this work He spoke in the answer He sent to John the Baptist. John was in prison, and had become despondent; he was even troubled by doubts as to whether Jesus was really the Messiah. So he sent some of his followers to ask the Saviour:

"Art Thou He that should come, or do we look for another?"

When the messengers came to Jesus, there were about Him many sick, whom He was healing. All day the messengers waited, while He worked with tireless activity to help the suffering ones. At last He said:

"Go and show John again those things which ye do hear and see: the blind receive their sight, and the lame walk, the lepers are cleansed, and the deaf hear, the dead are raised up, and the poor have the gospel preached to them." Matthew 11:3-5.

So, for three years and a half, Jesus "went about doing good." Then the time came for His ministry on earth to be finished. With His disciples He must go up to Jerusalem to be betrayed, condemned, and crucified.

Thus were to be fulfilled His own words, "The Good Shepherd giveth His life for the sheep." John 10:11.

"Surely He hath borne our griefs, and carried our sorrows. . . . He was wounded for our transgressions, He was bruised for our iniquities: the chastisement of our peace was upon Him; and with His stripes we are healed. All we like sheep have gone astray; we have turned every one to his own way; and the Lord hath laid on Him the iniquity of us all." Isaiah 53:4-6.

The Good Shepherd
Finds the Lost Sheep

Jesus is the Good Shepherd and we are the sheep
of His pasture. When a lamb is lost, He hunts for
it until He finds it.

PAINTING BY CLYDE PROVONSHA

THE NINETY AND NINE

There were ninety and nine that safely lay
    In the shelter of the fold,
But one was out on the hills away,
    Far, far from the gates of gold—
Away on the mountains wild and bare,
Away from the tender Shepherd's care.

"Lord, Thou hast here Thy ninety and nine;
    Are they not enough for Thee?"
But the Shepherd made answer: "One of Mine
    Has wandered away from Me,
And although the road be rough and steep,
I go to the desert to find My sheep."

But none of the ransomed ever knew
    How deep were the waters crossed,
Nor how dark was the night that the Lord passed through
    Ere He found His sheep that was lost.
Far out in the desert He heard its cry—
Fainting and helpless and ready to die.

"Lord, whence are these blood drops all the way
    That mark out the mountain's track?"
"They were shed for one who had gone astray,
    Ere the Shepherd could bring him back."
"Lord, why are Thy hands so rent and torn?"
"They are pierced tonight by many a thorn."

But all through the mountains, thunder-riven,
    And up from the rocky steep,
There rose a cry to the gate of heaven,
    "Rejoice, I have found My sheep!"
And the angels sang around the throne,
"Rejoice, for the Lord brings back His own!"
                —ELIZABETH C. CLEPHANE.

H. HOFMANN

The kingly welcome which Jesus received as He neared Jerusalem on His way to the Passover feast brought His mission to the attention of the whole Jewish nation and fulfilled an ancient prophecy concerning Him.

Riding Into Jerusalem

*J*ESUS was nearing Jerusalem to attend the Passover. He was surrounded by multitudes who were also going up to this great yearly feast.

At His command, two of the disciples brought an ass's colt that He might ride into Jerusalem. They spread their garments upon the beast, and placed their Master upon it.

As soon as He was seated, a loud shout of triumph rent the air. The multitude hailed Him as Messiah, their King. More than five hundred years before, the prophet had foretold this scene:

"Rejoice greatly, O daughter of Zion; . . . behold, thy King cometh unto thee; . . . lowly, and riding upon an ass, and upon a colt the foal of an ass." Zechariah 9:9.

All in the rapidly increasing throng were happy and excited. They could not offer Him costly gifts, but they spread their outer garments, as a carpet, in His path.

They broke off the beautiful branches of the olive and the palm, and strewed them in the way. They thought they were escorting Christ to take possession of the throne of David in Jerusalem.

The Saviour had never before allowed His followers to show Him kingly honors. But at this time He desired especially to manifest Himself to the world as its Redeemer.

The Son of God was about to become a sacrifice for the sins of men. His church in all succeeding ages must make His death a subject of deep thought and study. It was necessary, then, that the eyes of all people should now be directed to Him.

After such a scene as this, His trial and crucifixion could never be hidden from the world. It was God's design that each event in the closing days of the Saviour's life should be so plainly marked that no power could cause it to be forgotten.

In the vast multitude surrounding the Saviour were the evidences of His miracle-working power.

The blind whom He had restored to sight were leading the way.

The dumb whose tongues He had loosed, shouted the loudest hosannas.

The cripples whom He had healed leaped for joy, and were most active in breaking the palm branches and waving them before Him.

Widows and orphans were exalting the name of Jesus for His works of mercy to them.

The loathsome lepers who had been cleansed by a word, spread their garments in the way.

Those who had been raised from the dead by the life-giving voice of the Saviour were there.

And Lazarus, whose body had seen corruption in the grave, but who was now enjoying the strength of glorious manhood, was with the happy throng that escorted the Saviour to Jerusalem.

As new numbers were added to the throng, they caught the inspiration of the hour, and joined in the shouts that echoed and re-echoed from hill to hill and from valley to valley:

"Hosanna to the Son of David!   Blessed is He that cometh in the name of the Lord! Hosanna in the highest." Matthew 21:9.

Many Pharisees witnessed this scene, and were displeased. They felt that they were losing the control of the people. With all their authority they tried to silence them; but their threats and appeals only increased the enthusiasm.

Finding that they could not control the people, they pressed through the crowd to where Jesus was, and said to Him: "Master, rebuke Thy disciples."

They declared that such a tumult was unlawful, and would not be permitted by the rulers.

Jesus said, "I tell you that, if these should hold their peace, the stones would immediately cry out." Luke 19:39, 40.

This scene of triumph was of God's own appointing; it had been foretold by the prophets, and no earthly power could stop it. The work of God will ever go forward, in spite of all that man may do to hinder it or tear it down.

As the procession came to the brow of the hill overlooking Jerusalem, the full splendor of the city met their view.

The vast multitude hushed their shouts, spellbound by the sudden vision of beauty. All eyes turned upon the Saviour, expecting to see in His countenance the admiration which they themselves felt.

Jesus halted, and a cloud of sorrow gathered upon His countenance, and the multitude were astonished to see Him burst into an agony of weeping.

Those who surrounded the Saviour could not understand His grief; but He wept for the city that was doomed.

It had been the child of His care, and His heart was filled with anguish as He realized that it would soon be made desolate.

Had her people given heed to Christ's teaching, and received Him as the Saviour, Jerusalem would have "stood forever."

She might have become the queen of kingdoms, free in the strength of her God-given power.

There would then have been no armed soldiers waiting at her gates, no Roman banners waving from her walls.

From Jerusalem the dove of peace would have gone to all nations. She would have been the crowning glory of the world.

But the Jews had rejected their Saviour; they were about to crucify their King. And when the sun should set that night, the doom of Jerusalem would be forever sealed. (About forty years afterward, Jerusalem was utterly destroyed and burned with fire by the Roman army.)

Reports had come to the rulers that Jesus was nearing the city with a vast company of followers. They went out to meet Him, hoping to scatter the throng. With a show of much authority they asked: "Who is this?" Matthew 21:10.

The disciples, filled with the Spirit of inspiration, answered: "Adam will tell you, 'It is the Seed of the woman that shall bruise the serpent's head.'

"Ask Abraham. He will tell you, 'It is Melchisedek, King of Salem, King of Peace.'

"Jacob will tell you, 'He is Shiloh of the tribe of Judah.'

"Isaiah will tell you, 'Immanuel, Wonderful, Counsellor, the mighty God, the everlasting Father, the Prince of Peace.'

"Jeremiah will tell you, 'The Branch of David, the Lord, our righteousness.'

"Daniel will tell you, 'He is the Messiah.'

"Hosea will tell you, 'He is the Lord God of Hosts, the Lord is His memorial.'

"John the Baptist will tell you, 'He is the Lamb of God that taketh away the sin of the world.'

"The great Jehovah has proclaimed from His throne, 'This is My beloved Son.'

"We, His disciples, declare, 'This is Jesus, the Messiah, the Prince of Life, the Redeemer.'

"And even the prince of the power of darkness acknowledges Him, saying, 'I know Thee who Thou art, the Holy One of God!' "

Jesus drove the traders and the money-changers from the temple and said sternly,
"Make not My Father's house a house of merchandise."

"Take These Things Hence"

THE NEXT day Christ entered the temple. Three years before, He had found men buying and selling in the outer court, and had rebuked them and driven them out.

Now as He came again to the temple, He found the same traffic still carried on. The court was filled with cattle, sheep, and birds. These were sold to those who wished to offer sacrifice for their sins.

Extortion and robbery were practiced by those engaged in this traffic. So great was the babel of sounds from the court, that it seriously disturbed the worshipers within.

Christ stood on the steps of the temple, and again His piercing gaze swept over the court. All eyes were turned toward Him. The voices of the people and the noise of the cattle were hushed. All looked with astonishment and awe upon the Son of God.

The divine flashed through the human, and gave Jesus a dignity and glory He had never manifested before. The silence became almost unbearable.

At last He said in clear tones, and with a power that swayed the people like a mighty tempest:

"It is written, My house is the house of prayer: but ye have made it a den of thieves." Luke 19:46.

With still greater authority than He had manifested three years before, He commanded:

"Take these things hence."

Once before the priests and rulers of the temple had fled at the sound of this voice. Afterward they were ashamed of their fear. They felt that they would never flee in this way again.

Yet they were now more terrified, and in greater haste than before to obey His command, and they rushed from the temple, driving their cattle before them.

Soon the court was filled with people who brought their sick to be healed by Jesus. Some were dying. These afflicted ones felt their distressing need.

They fixed their eyes imploringly upon the face of Christ, fearing to see there the severity which had driven out the buyers and sellers. But they saw in His face only love and tender pity.

Jesus kindly received the sick, and disease and suffering fled at the touch of His hand. He tenderly gathered the children in His arms, soothed their fretful cries, banished sickness and pain from their little forms, and handed them back, smiling and healthy, to their mothers.

What a scene to greet the priests and rulers as they cautiously made their way back to the temple! They heard the voices of men, women, and children praising God.

They saw the sick healed, the blind restored to sight, the deaf receive their hearing, and the lame leap for joy.

The children took the lead in these rejoicings. They repeated the hosannas of the day before, and waved palm branches before the Saviour. The temple echoed and re-echoed with their shouts:

"Hosanna to the Son of David:

"Blessed is He that cometh in the name of the Lord!" Matthew 21:9.

"Behold, thy King cometh unto thee: He is just, and having salvation." Zechariah 9:9.

The rulers tried to silence the shouts of the happy children, but all were filled with joy and praise for the wonderful works of Jesus, and they would not be silenced.

The rulers then turned to the Saviour, hoping that He would command them to cease. They said to Him:

"Hearest Thou what these say?"

Jesus replied, "Yea; have ye never read, Out of the mouth of babes and sucklings Thou hast perfected praise?" Matthew 21:16.

The blessed privilege of heralding the birth of Christ and forwarding His work in the earth had been refused by the haughty rulers of the people.

His praises must be sounded; and God chose the children to do it. Had the voices of these rejoicing children been silenced, the very pillars of the temple would have cried out in the Saviour's praise.

The last Passover supper which Jesus ate with His disciples was filled with meaning
both for them and for us today, for Jesus Himself was the true Passover Lamb.

At the Passover Supper

*T*HE CHILDREN of Israel ate the first Passover supper at the time of their release from bondage in Egypt.

God had promised to set them free. He had told them that the first-born son in every family of the Egyptians was to be slain.

He had told them to mark their own door posts with the blood of the slain lamb, that the angel of death might pass them by.

The lamb itself they were to roast and eat at night, with unleavened bread and with bitter herbs, which represented the bitterness of their slavery.

When they ate the lamb, they must be all ready for a journey. They must have their shoes on their feet, and their staves in their hands.

They did as the Lord had said, and that very night the king of Egypt sent them word that they might go free. In the morning they started on their way to the land of promise.

So every year, the same night on which they left Egypt,

all the Israelites kept the feast of the Passover at Jerusalem. At this feast each family had a roasted lamb, with bread and bitter herbs, as their forefathers had in Egypt. And they told their children the story of God's goodness in freeing His people from slavery.

The time had now come when Christ was to keep the feast with His disciples, and He told Peter and John to find a place, and make ready the Passover supper.

A great many people came to Jerusalem at this time, and those who lived in the city were always ready to give a room in their houses for visitors to keep the feast.

The Saviour told Peter and John that when they had gone into the street, they would meet a man carrying a pitcher of water. Him they were to follow, and they were to go into the house where he went. And they were to say to the good man of that house:

"The Master saith unto thee, Where is the guestchamber, where I shall eat the Passover with My disciples?"

This man would then show them a large upper room furnished for their needs; there they were to prepare the Passover supper. And it all happened just as the Saviour had told them it would.

At the Passover supper the disciples were alone with Jesus. The time they spent with Him at these feasts had always been a time of joy; but now He was troubled in spirit.

At last He said to them in tones of touching sadness:

"With desire I have desired to eat this Passover with you before I suffer."

There was sweet wine on the table, and He took a cup of it, "and gave thanks, and said:

"Take this, and divide it among yourselves: for I say unto you, I will not drink of the fruit of the vine, until the kingdom of God shall come." Luke 22:11, 15, 17, 18.

This was the last time that Christ was to keep the feast with His disciples. It was really the last Passover that was ever to be kept. For the lamb was slain to teach the people about Christ's death; and when Christ, the Lamb of God, should be slain for the sins of the world, there would be no need of slaying a lamb to represent His death.

When the Jews sealed their rejection of Christ by putting Him to death, they rejected all that gave to this feast its value and significance. Henceforth its observance by them was a worthless form.

As Christ joined in the Paschal service, there was before His mind the scene of His last great sacrifice. He was now in the shadow of the cross, and the pain was torturing His heart. He knew all the anguish that awaited Him.

He knew the ingratitude and cruelty that would be shown Him by those He had come to save. But it was not of His own suffering that He thought. He pitied those who would reject their Saviour and lose eternal life.

And the thought of His disciples was uppermost in His mind. He knew that after His own suffering was over, they would be left to struggle in the world.

He had much to tell them that would be a stay to their hearts when He should walk no more with them. Of these things He had hoped to speak at this their last meeting before His death.

But He could not tell them now. He saw that they were not ready to listen.

There had been a contention among them. They still

F. BROWN

Jesus gave us a wonderful example of humility and love when He acted the part of a servant and washed the disciples' feet.

thought that Christ was soon to be made king, and each of them wanted the highest place in His kingdom. So they had jealous and angry feelings toward one another.

There was another cause of trouble. At a feast it was the custom for a servant to wash the feet of the guests, and on this occasion preparation had been made for the service. The pitcher of water, the basin, and the towel were there, ready for the feet-washing. But no servant was present, and it was the disciples' part to perform it.

But each of the disciples thought that he would not be a servant to his brethren. He was not willing to wash their feet. So, in silence they had taken their places at the table.

Jesus waited awhile to see what they would do. Then He Himself rose from the table. He girded Himself with the towel, poured water into the basin, and began to wash the disciples' feet. He had been grieved by their contention, but He did not reprove them by sharp words. He showed His love by acting as a servant to His own disciples. When He had finished, He said to them:

"If I then, your Lord and Master, have washed your feet; ye also ought to wash one another's feet. For I have given you an example that ye should do as I have done to you." John 13:14, 15.

In this way Christ taught them that they ought to help one another. Instead of seeking the highest place for himself, each should be willing to serve his brethren.

The Saviour came into the world to work for others. He lived to help and save those who are needy and sinful. He wants us to do as He did.

The disciples were now ashamed of their jealousy and selfishness. Their hearts were filled with love for their Lord

7

and for one another. Now they could give heed to Christ's teaching.

As they were still at the table, Jesus took bread, and gave thanks, and broke it, and gave to them, saying, "This is My body which is given for you: this do in remembrance of Me.

"Likewise also the cup after supper, saying, This cup is the new testament in My blood, which is shed for you." Luke 22:19, 20.

The Bible says, "As often as ye eat this bread, and drink this cup, ye do show the Lord's death till He come." 1 Corinthians 11:26.

The bread and the wine represent the body and the blood of Christ. As the bread was broken, and the wine poured out, so on the cross Christ's body was broken, and His blood shed to save us.

By eating the bread and drinking the wine, we show that we believe this. We show that we repent of our sins, and that we receive Christ as our Saviour.

As the disciples sat at the table with Jesus, they saw that He still seemed greatly troubled. A cloud settled on them all, and they ate in silence.

At last Jesus spoke and said, "Verily I say unto you, that one of you shall betray Me."

The disciples were grieved and amazed at these words. Each began to look into his heart to see if there was any shadow of an evil thought against their Master.

One after another they asked, "Lord, is it I?"

Judas alone remained silent. This drew the eyes of all to him. When he saw that he was observed, he too asked, "Master, is it I?"

And Jesus solemnly replied, "Thou hast said." Matthew 26:21, 22, 25.

Jesus had washed the feet of Judas, but this had not caused him to love the Saviour more. He was angry that Christ should do a servant's work. Now he knew that Christ would not be made king, and he was the more determined to betray Him.

When he saw that his purpose was known, even this did not cause him to fear. In anger he quickly left the room, and went away to carry out his wicked plan. The going of Judas was a relief to all present. The Saviour's face lighted, and at this the shadow was lifted from the disciples.

Christ now talked for some time with His disciples. He was going to His Father's house, He said, to make a place ready for them, and He would come again to take them to Himself.

He promised to send the Holy Spirit to be their teacher and comforter while He was gone. He told them to pray in His name, and their prayers would surely be answered.

He then prayed for them, asking that they might be kept from evil, and might love one another as He had loved them.

Jesus prayed for us as well as for the first disciples. He said:

"Neither pray I for these alone, but for them also which shall believe on Me through their word; that they all may be one; as Thou, Father, art in Me, and I in Thee, that they also may be one in us: that the world may believe that Thou hast sent Me, . . . and hast loved them, as Thou hast loved Me." John 17:20-23.

CARL BLOCH

It was in the Garden of Gethsemane that Jesus really won the salvation of lost humanity. In the darkest hour of that dreadful night, an angel was sent to comfort and strengthen Him.

In Gethsemane

THE SAVIOUR'S life on earth was a life of prayer. Many were the hours He spent alone with God. Often did He send up His earnest petitions to His heavenly Father. Thus He received strength and wisdom to sustain Him in His work, and to keep Him from falling under the temptations of Satan.

After eating the Passover supper with His disciples, Jesus went with them to the garden of Gethsemane, where He often went to pray. As He walked, He talked with them, and taught them; but as they neared the garden, He became strangely silent.

All His life, Jesus had lived in the presence of His Father. The Spirit of God had been His constant guide and support. He always gave God the glory for His works on earth, and said, "I can of Mine own self do nothing." John 5:30.

We can do nothing of ourselves. It is only by relying on Christ for all our strength that we can overcome, and do His will on earth. We must have the same simple, childlike trust in Him that He had in His Father. Christ said, "Without Me ye can do nothing." John 15:5.

The terrible night of agony for the Saviour began as they neared the garden. It seemed that the presence of God, which had been His support, was no longer with Him. He was beginning to feel what it was to be shut out from His Father.

Christ must bear the sins of the world. As they were now laid upon Him, they seemed more than He could endure. The guilt of sin was so terrible, He was tempted to fear that God could no longer love Him.

As He felt the awful displeasure of the Father against evil, the words were forced from Him, "My soul is exceeding sorrowful, even unto death."

Near the gate of the garden, Jesus had left all His disciples except Peter, James, and John, and He had gone into the garden with these three. They were His most earnest followers, and had been His closest companions. But He could not bear that even they should witness the suffering He was to endure. He said to them:

"Tarry ye here, and watch with Me." Matthew 26:38.

He went a short distance from them, and fell prostrate upon the ground. He felt that by sin He was being separated from the Father. The gulf between them appeared so broad, so black, so deep, that He shuddered before it.

Christ was not suffering for his own sins, but for the sins of the world. He was feeling the displeasure of God against sin as the sinner will feel it in the great judgment day.

In His agony, Christ clung to the cold ground. From His pale lips came the bitter cry, "O My Father, if it be possible, let this cup pass from Me; nevertheless not as I will, but as Thou wilt." Matthew 26:39.

For an hour Christ bore this terrible suffering alone. Then He came to the disciples, hoping for some word of sympathy. But no sympathy awaited Him, for they were asleep. They awoke at the sound of His voice, but they hardly knew Him, His face was so changed by anguish. Addressing Peter, He said:

"Simon, sleepest thou? Couldest not thou watch one hour?" Mark 14:37.

Just before He bent His footsteps to the garden, Christ had said to the disciples, "All ye shall be offended because of Me this night." They had given Him the strongest assurance that they would go with Him to prison and to death. And poor, self-sufficient Peter had added, "Although all shall be offended, yet will not I." Mark 14:27, 29.

But the disciples trusted to themselves. They did not look to the Mighty Helper as Christ had counselled them to do. So when the Saviour was most in need of their sympathy and prayers, they were found asleep. Even Peter was sleeping.

And John, the loving disciple who had leaned upon the breast of Jesus, was asleep. Surely the love of John for his Master should have kept him awake. His earnest prayers should have mingled with those of his loved Saviour in the time of His great agony. The Redeemer had spent whole nights in praying for His disciples, that their faith might not fail in the hour of trial. Yet they could not remain awake with Him even one hour.

Had Christ now asked James and John, "Can ye drink of the cup that I drink of? and be baptized with the baptism that I am baptized with?" they would not have answered so readily as they did before, "We can." Mark 10:38, 39.

The Saviour's heart was filled with pity and sympathy at the weakness of His disciples. He feared that they could not endure the test which His suffering and death would bring upon them.

Yet He did not sternly reprove them for their weakness. He thought of the trials that were before them, and said:

"Watch and pray, that ye enter not into temptation."

He made an excuse for their failure in duty toward Him: "The spirit indeed is willing, but the flesh is weak." Matthew 26:41. What an example of the tender, loving pity of the Saviour!

Again the Son of God was seized with superhuman agony. Fainting and exhausted, He staggered back, and prayed as He had prayed before:

"O My Father, if this cup may not pass away from Me, except I drink it, Thy will be done." Matthew 26:42.

The agony of this prayer forced drops of blood from His pores. Again He sought the disciples for sympathy, and again He found them sleeping. His presence aroused them. They looked upon His face with fear, for it was stained with blood. They could not understand the anguish of mind which His face expressed.

The third time He sought the place of prayer. A horror of great darkness overcame Him. He had lost the presence of His Father. Without this, He feared that in His human nature He could not endure the test.

The third time He prays the same prayer as before. Angels long to bring relief, but it may not be. The Son of

God must drink this cup, or the world will be lost forever. He sees the helplessness of man. He sees the power of sin. The woes of a doomed world pass in review before Him.

He makes the final decision. He will save man at any cost to Himself. He has left the courts of Heaven, where all is purity, happiness, and glory, to save the one lost sheep, the one world that has fallen by transgression, and He will not turn from His purpose. His prayer now breathes only submission:

"If this cup may not pass away from Me, except I drink it, Thy will be done."

The Saviour now falls dying to the ground. No disciple is there, to place his hand tenderly beneath his Master's head, and bathe that brow, marred indeed more than the sons of men. Christ is alone; of all the people there are none with Him.

But God suffers with His Son. Angels behold the Saviour's agony. There is silence in Heaven. No harp is touched. Could men have viewed the amazement of the angelic host as in silent grief they watched the Father separating His beams of light, love, and glory from His beloved Son, they would better understand how offensive in His sight is sin.

A mighty angel now comes to the side of Christ. He lifts the head of the divine sufferer upon his bosom, and points toward Heaven. He tells Him that He has come off victor over Satan. As the result, millions will be victors in His glorious kingdom.

A heavenly peace rests upon the Saviour's blood-stained face. He has borne that which no human being can ever bear; for He has tasted the sufferings of death for every man.

Again Christ sought His disciples, and again He found them sleeping. Had they remained awake, watching and praying with their Saviour, they would have received help for the trial before them. Missing this, they had no strength in their hour of need.

Looking sorrowfully on them, Christ said, "Sleep on now, and take your rest: behold, the hour is at hand, and the Son of man is betrayed into the hands of sinners."

Even as He spoke these words, He heard the footsteps of the mob in search of Him, and said:

"Rise, let us be going: behold, he is at hand that doth betray Me." Matthew 26:45, 46.

The Betrayal and Arrest

*N*O TRACES of His recent suffering were to be seen as the Saviour stepped forth to meet His betrayer. Standing in advance of His disciples, He asked the mob:

"Whom seek ye?"

They answered, "Jesus of Nazareth."

Jesus replied, "I am He." John 18:4, 5.

As Jesus spoke these words, the angel who had recently ministered to Him moved between Him and the mob. A divine light illuminated the Saviour's face, and a dovelike form overshadowed Him.

In the presence of this divine glory the murderous throng could not stand for a moment. They staggered back. The priests, elders, and soldiers dropped as dead men to the ground.

The angel withdrew, and the light faded away. Jesus could have escaped, but He remained, calm and self-possessed. His disciples were too much amazed to utter a word.

H. HOFMANN

Jesus could easily have resisted the betrayer's kiss. He could have destroyed His enemies with a word. But the words which He uttered were ones of sweet resignation to His Father's will.

The Roman soldiers soon started to their feet. With the priests and Judas, they gathered about Christ. They seemed ashamed of their weakness, and fearful that He would escape. Again the question was asked by the Redeemer: "Whom seek ye?"

Again they answered, "Jesus of Nazareth." The Saviour then said, "I have told you that I am He: if therefore ye seek Me, let these [pointing to His disciples] go their way." John 18: 7, 8.

In this hour of trial, Christ's thoughts were for His beloved disciples. He did not wish to have them suffer, even though He must go to prison and to death.

Judas, the betrayer, did not forget the part he was to act. He came to Jesus, and kissed Him.

Jesus said to him, "Friend, wherefore art thou come?" Matthew 26:50. His voice trembled as He added, "Betrayest thou the Son of man with a kiss?" Luke 22:48.

These gentle words should have touched the heart of Judas; but all tenderness and honor seemed to have left him. Judas had yielded himself to the control of Satan. He stood boldly before the Lord, and was not ashamed to give Him up to the cruel mob.

Christ did not refuse the traitor's kiss. In this He gave us an example of forebearance, love, and pity. If we are His disciples, we must treat our enemies as He treated Judas.

The murderous throng became bold as they saw Judas touch the form which had so recently been glorified before their eyes. They now laid hold of the Saviour, and bound those hands that had ever been employed in doing good.

The disciples did not think that Christ would allow Himself to be taken. They knew that the power which could strike down the mob as dead men could keep them helpless till Christ and His companions should escape.

They were disappointed and indignant as they saw the cords brought forward to bind the hands of Him whom they loved. Peter, in his anger, rashly drew his sword, and tried to defend his Master. But he only cut off an ear of the high priest's servant.

When Jesus saw what was done, He released His hands, though held firmly by the Roman soldiers, and saying, "Suffer ye thus far" (Luke 22:51), He touched the wounded ear, and it was instantly made whole.

He then said to Peter, "Put up again thy sword into his place: for all they that take the sword shall perish with the sword. Thinkest thou that I cannot now pray to My Father, and He shall presently give Me more than twelve legions of angels? But how then shall the Scriptures be fulfilled, that thus it must be?" Matthew 26:52-54. "The cup which My Father hath given Me, shall I not drink it?" John 18:11.

Christ then turned to the chief priests and the captains of the temple, who were with the mob, and said, "Are ye come out as against a thief, with swords and with staves to take me? I was daily with you in the temple teaching, and ye took Me not: but the Scriptures must be fulfilled." Mark 14:48, 49.

The disciples were offended when they saw that the Saviour made no effort to deliver Himself from His enemies. They blamed Him for not doing so. They could not understand His submission to the mob, and, terror-stricken, they forsook Him and fled.

Christ had foretold this desertion. "Behold," He had

said, "the hour cometh, yea, is now come, that ye shall be scattered, every man to his own, and shall leave Me alone: and yet I am not alone, because the Father is with Me." John 16:32.

The highest judges of the Jewish nation were not interested in giving justice as Jesus was brought before them. All they sought was some means of destroying the sinless Son of God.

Before Annas, Caiaphas, and the Sanhedrin

*J*ESUS was followed from the garden of Gethsemane by the hooting mob. He moved painfully, for His hands were tightly bound, and He was closely guarded.

He was taken first to the house of Annas, who had formerly been the high priest, but whose place was then filled by his son-in-law, Caiaphas. The wicked Annas had requested that he might be the first to see Jesus of Nazareth a bound captive. He hoped to draw from Him some evidence by which to secure His condemnation.

With this in view he questioned the Saviour with regard to His disciples and His teachings. Christ answered:

"I spake openly to the world; I ever taught in the synagogue, and in the temple, whither the Jews always resort; and in secret have I said nothing."

Then, turning upon the questioner, He said, "Why askest thou Me? Ask them which heard Me, what I have said." John 18:20, 21.

The priests themselves had set spies to watch Christ

8

and report His every word. Through these spies they knew of His sayings and of His works at every gathering of the people He had attended. The spies had sought to entrap Him in His words, that they might find something by which to condemn Him. So the Saviour said, "Ask them which heard Me." Go to your spies. They have heard what I have said. They can tell you what My teaching has been.

The words of Christ were so searching and pointed that the priest felt that his prisoner was reading his very soul.

But one of the servants of Annas, thinking that his master was not treated with proper respect, struck Jesus in the face saying: "Answerest Thou the high priest so?"

To this Jesus mildly said: "If I have spoken evil, bear witness of the evil: but if well, why smitest thou Me?" John 18:22, 23.

Christ could have summoned legions of angels from Heaven to His aid. But it was a part of His mission to endure in His humanity all the taunts and insults that men might heap upon Him.

From the house of Annas, the Saviour was taken to the palace of Caiaphas. He was to be tried before the Sanhedrin, and while its members were being called together, Annas and Caiaphas again questioned Him, but they gained no advantage.

When the members of the Sanhedrin had assembled, Caiaphas took his seat as the president. On each side were the judges; before them stood the Roman soldiers guarding the Saviour; back of these was the accusing mob.

Caiaphas then bade Jesus work one of His mighty miracles before them. But the Saviour gave no sign that He heard a word. Had He responded by even one soul-searching look, such as He gave the buyers and sellers in the temple, the whole murderous throng would have been compelled to flee from His presence.

The Jews were at this time subject to the Romans, and were not allowed to punish any one with death. The Sanhedrin could only examine the prisoner, and pass judgment to be ratified by the Roman authorities.

To accomplish their wicked purpose, they must find something against the Saviour that would be regarded as criminal by the Roman governor. They could secure abundant evidence that Christ had spoken against the Jewish traditions and many of their ordinances. It was easy to prove that He had denounced the priests and scribes, and that He had called them hypocrites and murderers. But this would not be listened to by the Romans, for they themselves were disgusted with the pretensions of the Pharisees.

Many charges were brought against Christ, but either the witnesses disagreed, or the evidence was of such a nature that it would not be accepted by the Romans. They tried to make Him speak in answer to their accusations, but He appeared as if He had not heard them. The silence of Christ at this time had been thus described by the prophet Isaiah:

"He was oppressed, and He was afflicted, yet He opened not His mouth: He is brought as a lamb to the slaughter, and as a sheep before her shearers is dumb, so He openeth not His mouth." Isaiah 53:7.

The priests began to fear that they would fail of obtaining any evidence which they could bring against their prisoner before Pilate. They felt that one last effort must be made. The high priest raised his right hand toward Heaven, and addressed Jesus in the form of a solemn oath:

"I adjure Thee by the living God, that Thou tell us whether Thou be the Christ, the Son of God." Matthew 26:63.

The Saviour never denied His mission or His relation to the Father. He could remain silent to personal insult, but He ever spoke plainly and decidedly when His work or Sonship to God was called in question.

Every ear was bent to listen, and every eye was fixed upon Him as He answered: "Thou hast said."

In the custom of those days this was the same as answering, "Yes," or, "It is as thou hast said." This was the strongest form of an affirmative answer. A heavenly light seemed to illuminate the pale countenance of the Saviour as He added:

"Nevertheless I say unto you, Hereafter shall ye see the Son of man sitting on the right hand of power, and coming in the clouds of Heaven." Matthew 26:64.

In this statement the Saviour presented the reverse of the scene then taking place. He pointed forward to the time when He will occupy the position of supreme Judge of Heaven and earth. He will then be seated upon the Father's throne, and from His decisions there will be no appeal.

He brought before His hearers a view of that day, when, instead of being surrounded and abused by a riotous mob, He will come in the clouds of Heaven with power and great glory. Then He will be escorted by legions of angels. Then He will pronounce sentence upon His enemies, among whom will be that same accusing throng.

As Jesus spoke the words declaring Himself to be the Son of God, and Judge of the world, the high priest rent his robe, as if to show his horror. He lifted his hands toward Heaven, and said:

"He hath spoken blasphemy; what further need have we of witnesses? Behold, now ye have heard His blasphemy. What think ye?"

The judges answered, "He is guilty of death." Matthew 26:65, 66.

It was contrary to the Jewish law to try a prisoner by night. Though the condemnation of Christ had been determined, there must be a formal trial by day.

Jesus was taken to the guard room, and there suffered mockery and abuse from the soldiers and the rabble.

At daybreak He was again brought before His judges, and the final sentence of condemnation was pronounced.

A satanic fury then took possession of the leaders and the people. The roar of voices was like that of wild beasts. They made a rush for Jesus, crying, "He is guilty, put Him to death!" and had it not been for the soldiers, He would have been torn in pieces. But Roman authority interposed, and by force of arms restrained the violence of the mob.

Priests, rulers, and the rabble joined in abusing the Saviour. An old garment was thrown over His head; and His persecutors struck Him in the face, saying:

"Prophesy unto us, Thou Christ, Who is he that smote Thee?" Matthew 26:68.

When the garment was removed, one of the mocking throng spat in the Saviour's face.

The angels of God faithfully recorded every insulting

look, word, and act against their beloved Commander. One day those base men who scorned and spat upon the calm, pale face of Christ will look upon it in its glory, shining brighter than the sun.

Judas

THE JEWISH rulers had been anxious to get Jesus into their power, but for fear of raising a tumult among the people they had not dared to take Him openly. So they had sought some one who would secretly betray Him, and had found in Judas, one of the twelve disciples, the man who would do this base act.

Judas had naturally a strong love for money, but he had not always been wicked and corrupt enough to do such a deed as this. He had fostered the evil spirit of avarice until it had become the ruling motive of his life, and he could now sell his Lord for thirty pieces of silver (about $17.00), the price of a slave. (Exodus 21:28-32.) He could now betray the Saviour with a kiss in Gethsemane.

But he followed every step of the Son of God, as He went from the garden to the trial before the Jewish rulers. He had no thought that the Saviour would allow the Jews to kill Him, as they had threatened to do.

At every moment he expected to see Him released and protected by divine power, as had been done in the past.

Judas thought he was a clever businessman, but he traded love, happiness, and eternal life for a mere thirty pieces of silver. What a wretched bargain!

But as the hours went by, and Jesus quietly submitted to all the indignities that were heaped upon Him, a terrible fear came to the traitor, that he had indeed betrayed his Master to His death.

As the trial drew to a close, Judas could endure the torture of his guilty conscience no longer. All at once there rang through the hall a hoarse voice, which sent a thrill of terror to the hearts of all present:

"He is innocent. Spare Him, O Caiaphas. He has done nothing worthy of death!"

The tall form of Judas was seen pressing through the startled crowd. His face was pale and haggard, and large drops of sweat stood on his forehead. Rushing to the throne of judgment, he threw down before the high priest the pieces of silver that had been the price of his Lord's betrayal.

He eagerly grasped the robe of Caiaphas, and begged him to release Jesus, declaring that He had done no wrong. Caiaphas angrily shook him off, and said with scorn:

"What is that to us? See thou to that." Matthew 27:4.

Judas then threw himself at the Saviour's feet. He confessed that Jesus was the Son of God, and begged Him to deliver Himself from His enemies.

The Saviour knew that Judas did not really repent for what he had done. The false disciple feared that punishment would come upon him for his terrible deed; but he felt no real sorrow because he had betrayed the spotless Son of God.

Yet Christ spoke to him no word of condemnation. He looked with pity upon Judas, and said:

"For this hour came I into the world."

A murmur of surprise ran through the assembly. With amazement they beheld the forbearance of Christ toward His betrayer.

Judas saw that his entreaties were in vain, and he rushed from the hall, crying:

"It is too late! It is too late!"

He felt that He could not live to see Jesus crucified, and in despair went out and hanged himself.

Later that same day, on the road from Pilate's judgment hall to Calvary, the wicked throng were leading the Saviour to the place of crucifixion. Suddenly there came an interruption to their shouts and jeers. As they passed a retired spot, they saw at the foot of a lifeless tree the dead body of Judas.

It was a revolting sight. His weight had broken the cord by which he had hanged himself to the tree. In falling, his body had been horribly mangled, and the dogs were now devouring it.

His remains were immediately buried out of sight; but there was less mockery, and many a pale face revealed the fearful thoughts within. Retribution seemed already to be visiting those who were guilty of the blood of Jesus.

Before Pilate

*A*FTER Christ had been condemned by the judges of the Sanhedrin, He was taken at once to Pilate, the Roman governor, to have the sentence confirmed and executed.

The Jewish priests and rulers could not themselves enter the judgment hall of Pilate. By the ceremonial laws of their nation, they would become defiled by so doing, and thus be debarred from taking part in the feast of the Passover.

In their blindness they did not see that Christ was the real Passover lamb, and that since they had rejected Him, this great feast had for them lost its meaning.

As Pilate beheld Jesus, he saw a man of noble countenance and dignified bearing. No trace of crime was to be seen in His face. Pilate turned to the priests and asked:

"What accusation bring ye against this man?" John 18:29.

His accusers did not wish to state particulars, and so were not prepared for this question. They knew that they could bring no truthful evidence on which the Roman governor would condemn Him. So the priests called the false wit-

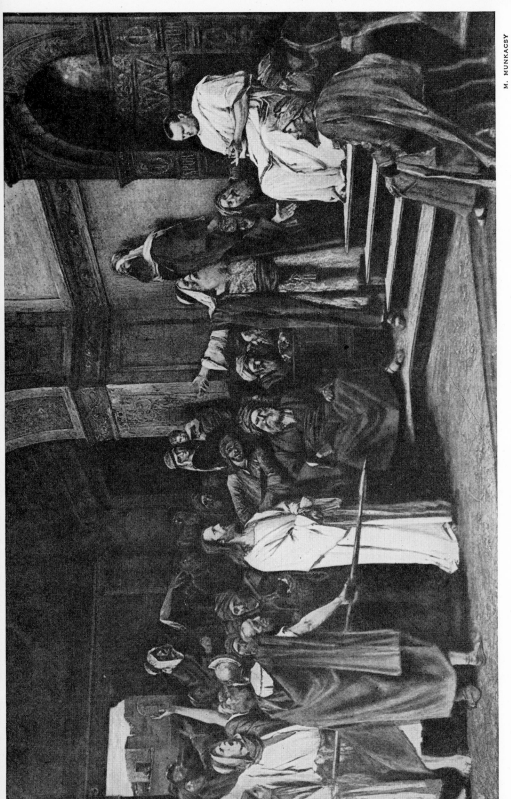

M. MUNKÁCSY

Pilate, the Roman governor, was a weak and selfish man. He knew that Jesus was innocent of any wrong, but fearing to offend the Jews, he sent the Son of God to His death.

nesses to their aid. "And they began to accuse Him, saying,

"We found this fellow perverting the nation, and forbidding to give tribute to Caesar, saying that He Himself is Christ a King." Luke 23:2.

This was false, for Christ had plainly sanctioned the payment of tribute to Caesar. When the lawyers had tried to entrap Him in regard to this very matter, He had said:

"Render therefore unto Caesar the things which are Caesar's." Matthew 22:21.

Pilate was not deceived by the testimony of the false witnesses. He turned to the Saviour, and asked:

"Art Thou the King of the Jews?"

Jesus answered, "Thou sayest." Matthew 27:11.

When they heard this answer, Caiaphas and those who were with him called Pilate to witness that Jesus had admitted the crime of which they accused Him. With noisy cries they demanded that He be sentenced to death.

As Christ made no answer to His accusers, Pilate said to Him: "Answerest Thou nothing? Behold how many things they witness against Thee.

"But Jesus yet answered nothing." Mark 15:4, 5.

Pilate was perplexed. He saw no evidence of crime in Jesus, and he had no confidence in those who were accusing Him. The noble appearance and quiet manner of the Saviour were in direct contrast to the excitement and fury of His accusers. Pilate was impressed with this, and was well satisfied of His innocence.

Hoping to gain the truth from Him, he took Jesus by Himself, and questioned Him: "Art Thou the King of the Jews?"

Christ did not give a direct answer to this question, but

asked: "Sayest thou this thing of thyself, or did others tell it thee of Me?"

The Spirit of God was striving with Pilate. The question of Jesus was intended to lead him to examine his own heart more closely. Pilate understood the meaning of the question. His own heart was opened before him, and he saw that his soul was stirred by conviction. But pride arose in his heart, and he answered:

"Am I a Jew? Thine own nation and the chief priests have delivered Thee unto me: what hast Thou done?"

Pilate's golden opportunity had passed. But Jesus desired Pilate to understand that He had not come to be an earthly king, therefore He said:

"My kingdom is not of this world: if My kingdom were of this world, then would My servants fight, that I should not be delivered to the Jews: but now is My kingdom not from hence."

Pilate then asked, "Art Thou a king then?"

Jesus answered, "Thou sayest that I am a king. To this end was I born, and for this cause came I into the world, that I should bear witness unto the truth. Every one that is of the truth heareth My voice."

Pilate had a desire to know the truth. His mind was confused. He eagerly grasped the words of the Saviour, and his heart was stirred with a great longing to know what the truth really was, and how he could obtain it. He asked Jesus: "What is truth?"

But he did not wait to receive an answer. The tumult of the crowd outside the hall of justice had increased to a roar. The priests were clamorous for immediate action, and Pilate was recalled to the interests of the hour. Going out

to the people, he declared: "I find in Him no fault at all."
John 18:33-38.

These words from a heathen judge were a scathing rebuke
to the base perfidy and falsehood of the rulers of Israel who
were accusing the Saviour.

As the priests and elders heard this from Pilate, their
disappointment and rage knew no bounds. They had long
plotted and waited for this opportunity. As they saw the
prospect of the release of Jesus, they seemed ready to tear
Him in pieces.

They lost all reason and self-control, and gave vent to
curses, behaving more like demons than like men. They
loudly denounced Pilate, and threatened him with the cen-
sure of the Roman government. They accused Pilate of
refusing to condemn Jesus, who, they affirmed, had set
Himself up against Caesar. Then they raised the cry:

"He stirreth up the people, teaching throughout all
Jewry, beginning from Galilee to this place." Luke 23:5.

Pilate at this time had no thought of condemning Jesus.
He was sure of His innocence. But when he heard that
Christ was from Galilee, he decided to send Him to Herod,
the ruler of that province, who was then in Jerusalem. By
this course Pilate thought to shift the responsibility of the
trial from himself to Herod.

Jesus was faint from hunger, and weary from loss of
sleep. He was also suffering from the cruel treatment He
had received. But Pilate delivered Him again to the soldiers, and He was dragged away, amid the jeers and insults
of the merciless mob.

H. HOFMANN.

Satan tried desperately through the brutality of wicked men to cause Jesus to sin.
But all the fearful abuse heaped upon Him failed to produce one unguarded word
from His lips.

Before Herod

*H*EROD had never met Jesus, but he had long desired to see Him, and to witness His marvelous power. As the Saviour was brought before him, the rabble surged and pressed about, some crying one thing, and some another. Herod commanded silence, for he wished to question the prisoner.

He looked with curiosity and pity upon the pale face of Christ. He saw there the marks of deep wisdom and purity. He was satisfied, as Pilate had been, that malice and envy alone had caused the Jews to accuse the Saviour.

Herod urged Christ to perform one of His wonderful miracles before him. He promised to release Him if He would do so. By his direction, crippled and deformed persons were brought in, and he commanded Jesus to heal them. But the Saviour stood before Herod as one who neither saw nor heard.

The Son of God had taken upon Himself man's nature. He must do as man must do in similar circumstances. Therefore He would not work a miracle to gratify curiosity, or to save Himself from the pain and humiliation that man must endure when placed in a similar position.

His accusers were terrified when Herod demanded of Christ a miracle. Of all things they dreaded most an exhibition of His divine power. Such a manifestation would be a death blow to their plans, and would perhaps cost them their lives. So they set up the cry that Jesus worked miracles through the power given Him by Beelzebub, the prince of the devils.

Several years before this, Herod had listened to the teaching of John the Baptist. He had been deeply impressed, but he had not forsaken his life of intemperance and sin. So his heart grew harder, and at last in a drunken revel he had commanded that John should be slain to please the wicked Herodias.

Now he had become still more hardened. He could not bear the silence of Jesus. His face grew dark with passion, and he angrily threatened the Saviour, who still remained unmoved and silent.

Christ had come into the world to heal the broken-hearted. Could He have spoken any word to heal the bruises of sin-sick souls, He would not have kept silent. But He had no words for those who would but trample the truth under their unholy feet.

The Saviour might have spoken to Herod words that would have pierced the ears of the hardened king. He might have stricken him with fear and trembling by laying before him the full iniquity of his life, and the horror of his approaching doom. But Christ's silence was the severest rebuke that He could have given.

That ear which had ever been open to the cry of human

woe, had no place for the command of Herod. That heart, ever touched by the plea of even the worst sinners, was closed to the haughty king who felt no need of a Saviour.

In anger, Herod turned to the multitude, and denounced Jesus as an imposter. But the accusers of the Saviour knew that He was no imposter. They had seen too many of His mighty works to believe this charge.

Then the king began to shamefully abuse and ridicule the Son of God. "And Herod with his men of war set Him at naught, and mocked Him, and arrayed Him in a gorgeous robe." Luke 23:11.

As the wicked king saw Jesus accepting all this indignity in silence, he was moved with a sudden fear that this was no common man before him. He was perplexed with the thought that this prisoner might be a heavenly being come down to the earth.

Herod dared not ratify the condemnation of Jesus. He wished to relieve himself of the terrible responsibility, and so sent the Saviour back to Pilate.

G. DORÉ

Pilate's wife also believed Jesus to be innocent, and tried to influence her husband to release Him.

Condemned by Pilate

WHEN the Jews returned from Herod, bringing the Saviour again to Pilate, he was very much displeased, and asked what they would have him do. He reminded them that he had examined Jesus, and had found no fault in Him. He told them that they had brought complaints against Him, but that they had not been able to prove a single charge.

As stated in the preceding chapter, they had taken Him to Herod, who was a Jew, like themselves, and he had found in Him nothing worthy of death. But to pacify the accusers, Pilate said:

"I will therefore chastise Him, and release Him." Luke 23:16.

Here Pilate showed his weakness. He had acknowledged that Christ was innocent; then why should he punish Him? It was a compromise with wrong. The Jews never forgot this through all the trial. They had intimidated the Roman governor, and now pressed their advantage until they secured the condemnation of Jesus.

The multitude clamored more loudly for the life of the prisoner.

While Pilate was hesitating as to what he should do, there was brought to him a letter from his wife, which read:

"Have thou nothing to do with that just man: for I have suffered many things this day in a dream because of Him." Matthew 27:19.

Pilate turned pale at this message; but the mob became more urgent as they saw his indecision.

Pilate saw that something must be done. It was customary at the feast of the Passover to set at liberty one prisoner, whom the people might choose. The Roman soldiers had recently captured a noted robber, named Barabbas. He was a degraded ruffian and a murderer. So Pilate turned to the crowd, and said with great earnestness:

"Whom will ye that I release unto you? Barabbas, or Jesus which is called Christ?" Matthew 27:17.

They replied, "Away with this man, and release unto us Barabbas." Luke 23:18.

Pilate was dumb with surprise and disappointment. By yielding his own judgment and appealing to the people, he had lost his dignity and the control of the crowd. After that, he was only the tool of the mob. They swayed him at their will. He then asked:

"What shall I do then with Jesus which is called Christ?"

With one accord they cried, "Let Him be crucified.

"And the governor said, Why, what evil hath He done?

"But they cried out the more, saying, Let Him be crucified." Matthew 27:22, 23.

Pilate's cheek paled as he heard the terrible cry, "Let

Him be crucified." He had not thought it would come to that. He had repeatedly pronounced Jesus innocent, and yet the people were determined that He should suffer this most terrible and dreaded death. Again he asked the question:

"Why, what evil hath He done?"

And again was set up the awful cry, "Crucify Him, crucify Him."

Pilate made one last effort to touch their sympathies. Jesus was taken, faint with weariness and covered with wounds, and scourged in the sight of His accusers.

"And the soldiers platted a crown of thorns, and put it on His head, and they put on Him a purple robe, and said, Hail, King of the Jews! And they smote Him with their hands." John 19:2, 3.

They spit upon Him, and some wicked hand snatched the reed that had been placed in His hand, and struck the crown upon His brow, forcing the thorns into His temples, and sending the blood trickling down His face and beard.

Satan led the cruel soldiery in their abuse of the Saviour. It was his purpose to provoke Him to retaliation, if possible, or to drive Him to perform a miracle to release Himself, and thus break up the plan of salvation. One stain upon His human life, one failure of His humanity to bear the terrible test, and the Lamb of God would have been an imperfect offering, and the redemption of man a failure.

But He who could command the heavenly host, and in an instant call to His aid legions of holy angels, one of whom could have immediately overpowered that cruel mob —He who could have stricken down His tormentors by the

flashing forth of His divine majesty—submitted with dignified composure to the coarsest insult and outrage.

As the acts of His torturers degraded them below humanity, into the likeness of Satan, so did the meekness and
patience of Jesus exalt Him above humanity, and prove His
kinship to God.

Pilate was deeply moved by the uncomplaining patience
of the Saviour. He sent for Barabbas to be brought into
the court; then he presented the two prisoners side by side.
Pointing to the Saviour, he said in a voice of solemn en-
treaty, "Behold the man." "I bring Him forth to you,
that ye may know that I find no fault in Him." John 19:5, 4.

There stood the Son of God, wearing the robe of mockery and the crown of thorns. Stripped to the waist, His
back showed the long, cruel stripes from which the
blood flowed freely. His face was stained with blood,
and bore the marks of exhaustion and pain; but never
had it appeared more beautiful. Every feature expressed
gentleness and resignation, and the tenderest pity for His
cruel foes.

In striking contrast was the prisoner at His side. Every
line of the countenance of Barabbas showed him to be the
hardened ruffian that he was.

Among the beholders there were some who sympathized
with Jesus. Even the priests and rulers were convicted that
He was what He claimed to be. But they would not yield.
They had moved the mob to a mad fury, and again priests,
rulers, and people raised the cry:

"Crucify Him, crucify Him!"

At last, losing all patience with their unreasonable, venge-
ful cruelty, Pilate said to them:

"Take ye Him, and crucify Him: for I find no fault in Him." John 19:6.

Pilate tried hard to release the Saviour; but the Jews cried out:

"If thou let this man go, thou art not Caesar's friend: whosoever maketh himself a king speaketh against Caesar." John 19:12.

This was touching Pilate in a weak place. He was already under suspicion by the Roman government, and he knew that a report of this kind would be his ruin.

"When Pilate saw that he could prevail nothing, but that rather a tumult was made, he took water, and washed his hands before the multitude, saying,

"I am innocent of the blood of this just person: see ye to it." Matthew 27:24.

In vain Pilate tried to free himself from the guilt of condemning Jesus. Had he acted promptly and firmly at the first, carrying out his convictions of right, his will would not have been overborne by the mob; they would not have presumed to dictate to him.

His wavering and indecision proved his ruin. He saw that he could not release Jesus, and yet retain his own position and honor.

Rather than lose his worldly power, he chose to sacrifice an innocent life. Yielding to the demands of the mob, he again scourged Jesus, and delivered Him to be crucified.

But in spite of his precautions, the very thing he dreaded afterward came upon him. His honors were stripped from him, he was cast down from his high office, and, stung by remorse and wounded pride, not long after the crucifixion he ended his own life.

So all who compromise with sin will gain only sorrow and ruin. "There is a way which seemeth right unto a man, but the end thereof are the ways of death." Proverbs 14:12.

When Pilate declared himself innocent of the blood of Christ, Caiaphas answered defiantly, "His blood be on us, and on our children." Matthew 27:25.

And the awful words were echoed by the priests, and re-echoed by the people.

It was a terrible sentence to pass upon themselves. It was an awful heritage to hand down to their posterity.

Literally was this fulfilled upon themselves in the fearful scenes of the destruction of Jerusalem, about forty years later.

Literally has it been fulfilled in the scattered, despised, and oppressed condition of their descendants since that day.

Doubly literal will be the fulfillment when the final accounting shall come. The scene will then be changed, and "this same Jesus" will come, "in flaming fire taking vengeance on them that know not God." Acts 1:11; 2 Thessalonians 1:8.

Then they will pray to the rocks and mountains:

"Fall on us, and hide us from the face of Him that sitteth on the throne, and from the wrath of the Lamb: for the great day of His wrath is come." Revelation 6:16, 17.

Calvary

*J*ESUS was hurried to Calvary amid the shouts and jeers of the crowd. As He passed the gate of Pilate's court, the heavy cross which had been prepared for Barabbas was laid upon His bruised and bleeding shoulders. Crosses were placed also upon two thieves, who were to suffer death at the same time with Jesus.

The load was too heavy for the Saviour in His weary, suffering condition. He had gone but a few rods when He fell fainting beneath the cross.

When He revived, the cross was again placed upon His shoulders. He staggered on a few steps, and again fell to the ground as one lifeless. His persecutors now realized that it was impossible for Him to go farther with His burden, and they were puzzled to find someone who would carry the humiliating load.

Just then they were met by Simon a Cyrenian, coming from the opposite direction. Him they seized and compelled to carry the cross to Calvary.

The sons of Simon were disciples of Jesus, but he himself had not accepted the Saviour. Simon was ever after

139

As Jesus struggled under the weight of the cross on the way to execution, He turned
to the crying women who followed Him and said, "Weep not for me, but weep
for yourselves and for your children."

grateful for the privilege of bearing the cross of the Redeemer. The burden he was thus forced to carry became the means of his conversion. The events of Calvary and the words uttered by Jesus led Simon to accept Him as the Son of God.

Arriving at the place of crucifixion, the condemned were bound to the instruments of torture. The two thieves wrestled in the hands of those who stretched them upon the cross; but the Saviour made no resistance.

The mother of Jesus had followed Him on that awful journey to Calvary. She longed to minister to Him as He sank exhausted under His burden, but she was not allowed this privilege.

At every step of that wearisome way she had looked for Him to manifest His God-given power, and release Himself from the murderous throng. And now that the final scene was reached, and she saw the thieves bound to the cross, what an agony of suspense she endured!

Would He who had given life to the dead suffer Himself to be crucified? Would the Son of God suffer Himself to be thus cruelly slain? Must she give up her faith that He was the Messiah?

She saw His hands stretched upon the cross—those hands that had ever been reached out to bless the suffering. The hammer and the nails were brought, and as the spikes were driven through the tender flesh, the heartbroken disciples bore from the cruel scene the fainting form of the mother of Jesus.

The Saviour made no murmur of complaint; His face remained pale and serene, but great drops of sweat stood on His brow. His disciples had fled from the dreadful scene.

He was treading the winepress alone; and of the people there were none with Him. (Isaiah 63:3.)

As the soldiers were doing their work, the mind of Jesus passed from His own sufferings to the terrible retribution that His persecutors must one day meet. He pitied them in their ignorance, and prayed:

"Father, forgive them; for they know not what they do."

Christ was earning the right to become the advocate for men in the Father's presence. That prayer for His enemies embraced the world. It took in every sinner who had lived or should live, from the beginning of the world to the end of time.

Whenever we sin, Christ is wounded afresh. For us He lifts His pierced hands before the Father's throne, and says, "Forgive them; for they know not what they do."

As soon as Christ was nailed to the cross, it was lifted by strong men, and with great violence thrust into the place prepared for it. This caused intense suffering to the Son of God.

Pilate then wrote an inscription in Latin, Greek, and Hebrew, and placed it upon the cross, above the head of Jesus, where all might see it. It read:

"Jesus of Nazareth the King of the Jews."

The Jews requested that this might be changed. The chief priests said:

"Write not, The King of the Jews; but that He said, I am King of the Jews."

But Pilate was angry with himself because of his former weakness. He also thoroughly despised the jealous and wicked rulers. So he answered:

"What I have written I have written." John 19:22.

The soldiers divided the clothing of Jesus among themselves. One garment was woven without seam, and about this there was a contention. They finally settled the matter by casting lots. God's prophet had foretold that they would do this. He wrote:

"Dogs have compassed Me: the assembly of the wicked have inclosed Me: they pierced My hands and My feet. . . . They part My garments among them, and cast lots upon My vesture." Psalms 22:16, 18.

As soon as Jesus was lifted up on the cross, a terrible scene took place. Priests, rulers, and scribes joined with the rabble in mocking and jeering the dying Son of God, saying:

"If Thou be the King of the Jews, save Thyself." Luke 23:37.

"He saved others; Himself He cannot save. If He be the King of Israel, let Him now come down from the cross, and we will believe Him. He trusted in God; let Him deliver Him now, if He will have Him: for He said, I am the Son of God." Matthew 27:42, 43.

"And they that passed by railed on Him, wagging their heads, and saying, Ah, Thou that destroyest the temple, and buildest it in three days, save Thyself, and come down from the cross." Mark 15:29, 30.

Christ could have come down from the cross. But if He had done this, we could never have been saved. For our sake He was willing to die.

"He was wounded for our transgressions, He was bruised for our iniquities: the chastisement of our peace was upon Him; and with His stripes we are healed." Isaiah 53:5.

LOUIS FELDMANN

Jesus took our place upon the cross. He yielded up His precious life to make eternal life possible for all mankind. Such love is more than we can ever fully understand.

Death of Christ

*I*N YIELDING up His precious life, Christ was not upheld by triumphant joy. His heart was rent with anguish and oppressed with gloom. But it was not the fear or the pain of death that caused His suffering. It was the crushing weight of the sin of the world, a sense of separation from His Father's love. This was what broke the Saviour's heart, and brought His death so soon.

Christ felt the woe that sinners will feel when they awake to realize the burden of their guilt, to know that they have forever separated themselves from the joy and peace of Heaven.

Angels beheld with amazement the agony of despair borne by the Son of God. His anguish of mind was so intense that the pain of the cross was hardly felt.

Nature itself was in sympathy with the scene. The sun shone clearly until midday, when suddenly it seemed to be blotted out. All about the cross was darkness as deep as the blackest midnight. This supernatural darkness lasted fully three hours.

10

A nameless terror took possession of the multitude. The cursing and reviling ceased. Men, women, and children fell upon the earth in abject terror.

Lightnings occasionally flashed forth from the cloud, and revealed the cross and the crucified Redeemer. All thought that their time of retribution had come.

At the ninth hour the darkness lifted from the people, but still wrapped the Saviour as with a mantle. The lightnings seemed to be hurled at Him as He hung upon the cross. It was then that He sent up the despairing cry:

"My God, My God, why hast Thou forsaken Me?"

In the meantime the darkness had settled over Jerusalem and the plains of Judea. As all eyes were turned in the direction of the fated city, they saw the fierce lightnings of God's wrath directed toward it.

Suddenly the gloom was lifted from the cross, and in clear, trumpetlike tones, that seemed to resound throughout creation, Jesus cried:

"It is finished." John 19:30. "Father, into Thy hands I commend My spirit." Luke 23:46.

A light encircled the cross, and the face of the Saviour shone with a glory like the sun. He then bowed His head upon His breast and died.

The multitude about the cross stood paralyzed, and with bated breath gazed upon the Saviour. Again darkness settled upon the earth, and a hoarse rumbling like heavy thunder was heard. This was accompanied with a violent earthquake.

The people were shaken into heaps by the earthquake. The wildest confusion and terror ensued. In the surrounding mountains, rocks were rent asunder, and went crashing down into the plains below. Tombs were broken open, and many of the dead were cast out. Creation seemed to be breaking into atoms. Priests, rulers, soldiers, and people, mute with terror, were lying prostrate upon the ground.

At the time of the death of Christ, some of the priests were ministering in the temple at Jerusalem. They felt the shock of the earthquake, and at the same moment the vail of the temple, which separated the holy from the most holy place was rent in twain from top to bottom by the same bloodless hand that wrote the words of doom upon the walls of Belshazzar's palace. The most holy place of the earthly sanctuary was no longer sacred. Never would the presence of God again overshadow that mercy seat. Never would the acceptance or displeasure of God be manifested by the light or shadow in the precious stones in the breastplate of the high priest.

Henceforth the blood of the offerings in the temple was of no value. The Lamb of God, in dying, had become the sacrifice for the sins of the world.

When Christ died upon the cross of Calvary, the new and living way was thrown open to Jew and Gentile alike.

Angels rejoiced as the Saviour cried, "It is finished!" The great plan of redemption was to be carried out. Through a life of obedience, the sons of Adam might be exalted finally to the presence of God.

Satan was defeated, and knew that his kingdom was lost.

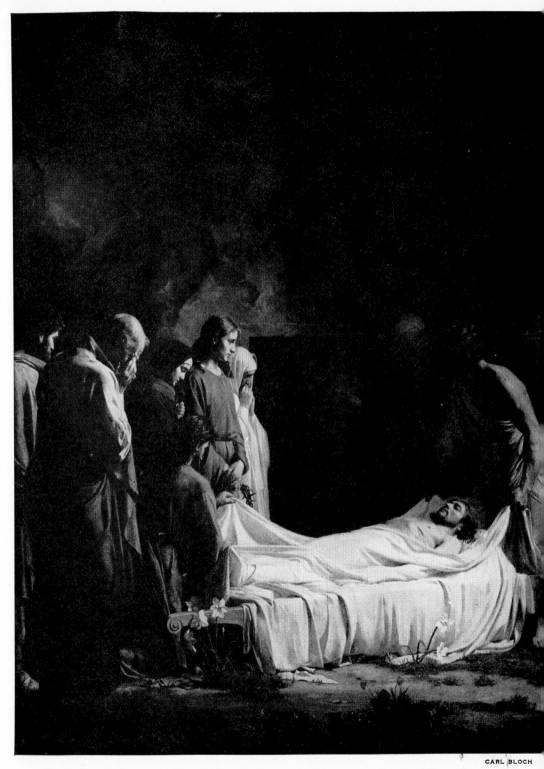

CARL BLOCH

Though Jesus was poor in this world's goods, the prophet had said He would make His grave with the rich. This was fulfilled when He was laid to rest in wealthy Joseph's new tomb.

In Joseph's Tomb

*T*REASON against the Roman government was the crime for which the Saviour was condemned. Persons put to death for this cause were buried in a place set apart for such criminals.

John shuddered at the thought of having the body of his beloved Master handled by the unfeeling soldiers, and buried in a dishonored grave. But he saw no way to prevent it, as he had no influence with Pilate.

At this trying time, Nicodemus and Joseph of Arimathaea came to the help of the disciples. Both of these men were members of the Sanhedrin, and were acquainted with Pilate. Both were men of wealth and influence. They were determined that the Saviour's body should have an honorable burial.

Joseph went boldly to Pilate, and begged from him the body of Jesus. Pilate, after learning that Christ was really dead, granted this request.

While Joseph was gone to Pilate for the Saviour's body, Nicodemus was making ready for the burial. It was the

149

custom in those times to wrap the bodies of the dead in linen cloths, with precious ointments and sweet spices. This was one method of embalming. So Nicodemus brought a costly gift of about a hundred pounds' weight of myrrh and aloes for the body of Jesus.

The most honored in all Jerusalem could not have been shown more respect in death. The humble followers of Jesus were astonished to see these wealthy rulers taking such an interest in the burial of their Master.

The disciples were overwhelmed with sorrow at the death of Christ. They forgot that He had told them it was to take place. They were without hope. Neither Joseph nor Nicodemus had openly accepted the Saviour while He was living. But they had listened to His teachings, and had closely watched every step of His ministry. Although the disciples had forgotten the Saviour's words foretelling His death, Joseph and Nicodemus remembered them well. And the scenes connected with the death of Jesus, which disheartened the disciples, and shook their faith, only proved to these rulers that He was the true Messiah, and led them to take their stand firmly as believers in Him.

The help of these rich and honored men was greatly needed at this time. They could do for their dead Master what it was impossible for the poor disciples to do.

Gently and reverently they, with their own hands, removed the body of Christ from the cross. Their tears of sympathy fell fast, as they looked upon His bruised and torn form.

Joseph owned a new tomb hewn in a rock. He had built it for his own use; but he now prepared it for Jesus. The body, together with the spices brought by Nicodemus, was wrapped in a linen sheet, and the Redeemer was borne to the tomb.

Although the Jewish rulers had succeeded in putting Christ to death, they could not rest easy. They well knew of His mighty power.

Some of them had stood by the grave of Lazarus, and had seen the dead brought back to life, and they trembled for fear that Christ would Himself rise from the dead, and again appear before them.

They had heard Him say to the multitude that He had power to lay down His life and to take it again.

They remembered that He had said, "Destroy this temple, and in three days I will raise it up" (John 2:19), and they knew that He was speaking of His own body.

Judas had told them that Christ had said to His disciples on their last journey to Jerusalem:

"Behold, we go up to Jerusalem; and the Son of man shall be betrayed unto the chief priests and unto the scribes, and they shall condemn Him to death, and shall deliver Him to the Gentiles to mock, and to scourge, and to crucify Him: and the third day He shall rise again." Matthew 20:18, 19.

They now remembered many things He had spoken which foretold His resurrection. They could not forget these things, however much they desired to do so. Like their father, the devil, they believed and trembled.

Everything declared to them that Jesus was the Son of God. They could not sleep, for they were more troubled about Him in death than they had been during His life.

Bent on doing all they could to keep Him in the grave, they asked Pilate to have the tomb sealed and guarded until the third day. Pilate placed a band of soldiers at the command of the priests, and said:

"Ye have a watch: go your way, make it as sure as ye can. So they went, and made the sepulcher sure, sealing the stone, and setting a watch." Matthew 27:65, 66.

He Is Risen

THE GREATEST care had been taken to guard the Saviour's tomb, and the entrance had been closed with a great stone. Upon this stone the Roman seal had been placed in such a way that the stone could not be moved without breaking the seal.

Around the tomb was the guard of Roman soldiers. They were to keep strict watch, that the body of Jesus might not be molested. Some of them were constantly pacing to and fro before the tomb, while the others rested on the ground near by.

But there was another guard around that tomb. Mighty angels from Heaven were there. Any one of this angel guard, by putting forth his power, could have stricken down the whole Roman army.

The night preceding the morning of the first day of the week has worn slowly away, and the darkest hour, just before daybreak, has come.

One of the most powerful angels is sent from Heaven. His countenance is like lightning, and his garments white

H. HOFMANN

On that glorious resurrection morning, Jesus came from the tomb a mighty victor over Satan and death. Because He lives, all who love and serve Him are assured of life eternal.

as snow. He parts the darkness from his track, and the whole heavens are lighted with his glory.

The sleeping soldiers awake, and start to their feet. With awe and wonder they gaze at the open heavens, and the vision of brightness which is nearing them.

The earth trembles and heaves as that powerful being from another world approaches. He is coming on a joyful errand, and the speed and power of his flight shake the world like a mighty earthquake. Soldiers, officers, and sentinels fall as dead men to the ground.

There had been still another guard about the Saviour's tomb. Evil angels were there. Because the Son of God had fallen in death, His body was even then claimed as the prey of him who has the power of death—the devil.

The angels of Satan were present to see that no power should take Jesus from their grasp. But as the mighty being sent from the throne of God approached, they fled in terror from the scene.

The angel laid hold of the great stone at the mouth of the tomb, and rolled it away, as if it had been but a pebble. Then with a voice that caused the earth to tremble, he cried:

"Jesus, Thou Son of God, come forth. Thy Father calls Thee!"

Then He who had earned the power over death and the grave came forth from the tomb. Above the rent sepulcher He proclaimed, "I am the resurrection, and the life." And the angel host bowed low in adoration before the Redeemer, and welcomed Him with songs of praise.

Jesus came forth with the tread of a conqueror. At His

presence the earth reeled, the lightning flashed, and the thunder rolled.

An earthquake marked the hour when Christ laid down His life. An earthquake also witnessed the moment when He took it up in triumph.

Satan was bitterly angry that his angels had fled at the approach of the heavenly messengers. He had dared to hope that Christ would not take up His life again, and that the plan of redemption was to fail. But as he saw the Saviour come forth from the tomb in triumph, all hope was lost. Satan now knew that his kingdom would have an end, and that he must finally be destroyed.

Go Tell My Disciples

*L*UKE, in his account of the Saviour's burial, speaks of the women who were with Him at His crucifixion, and says:

"They returned, and prepared spices and ointments; and rested the Sabbath day according to the commandment." Luke 23:56.

The Saviour was buried on Friday, the sixth day of the week. The women prepared spices and ointments with which to embalm their Lord, and laid them aside, until the Sabbath was past. Not even the work of embalming the body of Jesus would they do upon the Sabbath day.

"And when the Sabbath was past, . . . very early in the morning the first day of the week, they came unto the sepulcher at the rising of the sun." Mark 16:1, 2.

As they neared the garden, they were surprised to see the heavens beautifully lighted up, and to feel the earth trembling beneath their feet. They hastened to the tomb, and were still more astonished to find that the stone was rolled away, and that the Roman guard was not there.

157

B. PLOCKHORST

Mary was the first of the disciples to see the risen Jesus, and He instructed her to go
and tell the others the wonderful news.

Mary Magdalene had been the first to reach the place. Seeing that the stone was removed, she hurried away to tell the disciples. When the other women came up, they noticed a light shining about the tomb, and looking in, saw that it was empty.

As they lingered about the place, they suddenly beheld a young man in shining garments sitting by the tomb. It was the angel who had rolled away the stone. In fear they turned to flee, but the angel said:

"Fear not ye: for I know that ye seek Jesus, which was crucified. He is not here: for He is risen, as He said. Come, see the place where the Lord lay.

"And go quickly, and tell His disciples that He is risen from the dead; and, behold, He goeth before you into Galilee; there shall ye see Him." Matthew 28:5-7.

As the women looked again into the tomb, they saw another shining angel, who inquired of them:

"Why seek ye the living among the dead? He is not here, but is risen: remember how He spake unto you when He was yet in Galilee, saying, The Son of man must be delivered into the hands of sinful men, and be crucified, and the third day rise again." Luke 24:5-7.

The angels then explained the death and resurrection of Christ. They reminded the women of the words that Christ Himself had spoken, in which He had told beforehand of His crucifixion and His resurrection. These words of Jesus were now plain to them, and with fresh hope and courage they hastened away to tell the glad news.

Mary had been absent during this scene, but now returned with Peter and John. When they went back to Jerusalem, she stayed at the tomb. She could not bear to leave until she should learn what had become of the body of her Lord. As she stood weeping, she heard a voice which asked:

"Woman, why weepest thou? Whom seekest thou?"

Her eyes were so blinded by tears that she did not notice who it was that spoke to her. She thought it might be the gardener and said to him pleadingly:

"Sir, if thou have borne Him hence, tell me where thou hast laid Him, and I will take Him away."

She thought that if this rich man's tomb was considered too honorable a place for her Lord, she herself would provide a place for Him. But now the voice of Christ Himself fell upon her ears. He said:

"Mary."

Her tears were quickly brushed away, and she beheld the Saviour. Forgetting, in her joy, that He had been crucified, she stretched forth her hands to Him, saying:

"Rabboni" (Master).

Jesus then said, "Touch Me not; for I am not yet ascended to My Father: but go to My brethren, and say unto them, I ascend unto My Father, and your Father; and to My God, and your God." John 20:15-17.

Jesus refused to receive the homage of His people until He should know that His sacrifice had been accepted by the Father. He ascended to the heavenly courts, and from God Himself heard the assurance that His atonement for the sins of men had been ample, and through His blood all might gain eternal life.

All power in Heaven and on earth was given to the Prince of Life, and He returned to His followers in a world of sin, that He might impart to them His power and glory.

Witnesses

*L*ATE in the afternoon of the day of the resurrection, two of the disciples were on their way to Emmaus, a little town eight miles from Jerusalem.

They were perplexed over the events that had recently taken place, and especially concerning the reports of the women who had seen the angels, and had met Jesus after His resurrection.

They were now returning to their home, to meditate and pray, in hope of gaining some light in regard to those matters which were so dark to them.

As they journeyed, a stranger came up and went with them; but they were so busy with their conversation that they hardly noticed His presence.

These strong men were so burdened with grief that they wept as they traveled along. Christ's pitying heart of love saw here a sorrow which He could comfort.

Disguised as a stranger, He began to talk with them. "But their eyes were holden that they should not know Him. And He said unto them,

CARL BLOCH

As Jesus broke bread in the disciples' home at Emmaus, they saw the nail prints in His hands and realized with great astonishment that the stranger they had invited in was none other than Jesus, the Crucified One.

"What manner of communications are these that ye have one to another, as ye walk, and are sad?

"And the one of them, whose name was Cleopas, answering said unto Him,

"Art thou only a stranger in Jerusalem, and hast not known the things which are come to pass there in these days?

"And He said unto them, What things? And they said unto Him, Concerning Jesus of Nazareth, which was a prophet mighty in deed and word before God and all the people." Luke 24:16-19.

They then told what had taken place, and repeated the report brought by the women who had been at the tomb early that same morning. Then He said:

"O fools, and slow of heart to believe all that the prophets have spoken: Ought not Christ to have suffered these things, and to enter into His glory?

"And beginning at Moses and all the prophets, He expounded unto them in all the Scriptures the things concerning Himself." Luke 24:25-27.

The disciples were silent from amazement and delight. They did not venture to ask the stranger who He was. They listened eagerly as He explained to them Christ's mission.

Had the Saviour first made Himself known to the disciples, they would have been satisfied. In the fullness of their joy they would have desired nothing more. But it was necessary for them to understand how His mission had been foretold by all the types and prophecies of the Old Testament. Upon these their faith must be established. Christ performed no miracle to convince them, but it was

His first work to explain the Scriptures. They had looked upon His death as the destruction of all their hopes. Now He showed from the prophets that this was the very strongest evidence for their faith.

In teaching these disciples, Christ showed the importance of the Old Testament as a witness to His mission. Many now reject the Old Testament, claiming that it is no longer of any use. But such is not Christ's teaching. So highly did He value it, that at one time He said, "If they hear not Moses and the prophets, neither will they be persuaded, though one rose from the dead." Luke 16:31.

As the sun was setting, the disciples reached their home. Jesus "made as though He would have gone further." But the disciples could not bear to part from the One who had brought them such joy and hope.

So they said to Him, "Abide with us: for it is toward evening, and the day is far spent. And He went in to tarry with them." Luke 24:28, 29.

The simple evening meal was soon ready, and Christ took His place at the head of the table, as His custom was.

It was usually the duty of the head of the family to ask a blessing upon the food; but Christ placed His hands upon the bread and blessed it. And the eyes of the disciples were opened.

The act of blessing the food, the sound of the now familiar voice, the prints of the nails in His hands, all proclaimed Him their beloved Master.

For a moment they sat spellbound; then they arose to fall at His feet and worship Him; but He suddenly disappeared.

In their joy they forgot their hunger and weariness. They left the meal untasted, and hastened back to Jerusalem with the precious message of a risen Saviour.

As they were relating these things to the disciples, Christ Himself stood among them, and, with hands uplifted in blessing, said: "Peace be unto you." Luke 24:36.

At first they were frightened; but when He had shown them the prints of the nails in His hands and feet, and had eaten before them, they believed and were comforted. Faith and joy now took the place of unbelief, and with feelings which no words could express, they acknowledged their risen Saviour.

At this meeting, Thomas was not with them. He refused to believe the reports in regard to the resurrection. But after eight days Jesus appeared to the disciples when Thomas was present.

On this occasion He again showed in His hands and feet the marks of the crucifixion. Thomas was at once convinced, and cried, "My Lord and my God." John 20:28.

In the upper chamber, Christ again explained the Scriptures concerning Himself. Then He told His disciples that repentance and forgiveness of sins should be preached in His name among all nations, beginning at Jerusalem.

Before His ascension to Heaven, He said to them, "Ye shall receive power, after that the Holy Ghost is come upon you: and ye shall be witnesses unto Me both in Jerusalem, and in all Judea, and in Samaria, and unto the uttermost part of the earth." "And, lo, I am with you alway, even unto the end of the world." Acts 1:8; Matthew 28:20.

You have been witnesses, He said, of My life of self-sacrifice in behalf of the world. You have seen that all who come to Me, confessing their sins, I freely receive. All who will, may be reconciled to God, and have everlasting life.

To you, My disciples, I commit this message of mercy. It is to be given to all nations, tongues, and peoples.

Go to the farthest part of the habitable globe; but know that My presence will be there.

The Saviour's commission to the disciples included all the believers to the end of time.

Not all can preach to congregations; but all can minister to individuals. Those minister who receive the suffering, who help the needy, who comfort the sorrowing, and who tell the sinner of Christ's pardoning love. These are Christ's witnesses.

The Ascension

*T*HE SAVIOUR'S work on earth was finished. The time had now come for Him to return to His Heavenly home. He had overcome, and was again to take His place by the side of His Father upon His throne of light and glory.

Jesus chose the Mount of Olives as the place of His ascension. Accompanied by the eleven, He made His way to the mountain. But the disciples did not know that this was to be their last interview with their Master. As they walked, the Saviour gave them His parting instruction. Just before leaving them, He made that precious promise, so dear to every one of His followers:

"Lo, I am with you alway, even unto the end of the world." Matthew 28:20.

They crossed the summit, to the vicinity of Bethany. Here they paused, and the disciples gathered about their Lord. Beams of light seemed to radiate from His countenance as He looked with love upon them. Words of the deepest tenderness were the last which fell upon their ears from the lips of the Saviour.

167

ELSIE ANNA WOOD

As Jesus ascended to His Father, His promise echoed in their memory, "If I go, I will come again and receive you unto Myself."

With hands outstretched in blessing, He slowly ascended from among them. As He passed upward, the awe-stricken disciples looked with straining eyes for the last glimpse of their ascending Lord. A cloud of glory received Him from their sight. At the same time there floated down to them the sweetest and most joyous music from the angel choir.

While the disciples were still gazing upward, voices addressed them which sounded like richest music. They turned, and saw two angels in the form of men, who spoke to them, saying:

"Ye men of Galilee, why stand ye gazing up into Heaven? This same Jesus, which is taken up from you into Heaven, shall so come in like manner as ye have seen Him go into Heaven." Acts 1:11.

These angels belonged to the company that had come to escort the Saviour to His heavenly home. In sympathy and love for those left below, they had stayed to assure them that this separation would not be forever.

When the disciples returned to Jerusalem, the people looked upon them with amazement. After the trial and crucifixion of their Master, it had been thought that they would appear downcast and ashamed. Their enemies expected to see upon their faces an expression of sorrow and defeat. Instead of this, there was only gladness and triumph. Their faces were aglow with a happiness not born of earth. They did not mourn over disappointed hopes, but were full of praise and thanksgiving to God.

With rejoicing they told the wonderful story of Christ's resurrection and His ascension to heaven, and their testimony was received by many.

The disciples no longer had any distrust of the future.

They knew that the Saviour was in Heaven, and that His
sympathies were with them still. They knew that He was
pleading before God the merits of His blood. He was showing to the Father His wounded hands and feet, as an evidence of the price He had paid for His redeemed.

They knew that He would come again, with all the holy
angels with Him, and they looked for this event with great
joy and longing anticipation.

When Jesus passed from the sight of His disciples on
the Mount of Olives, He was met by a heavenly host, who,
with songs of joy and triumph, escorted Him upward.

At the portals of the city of God an innumerable company of angels await His coming. As Christ approaches
the gates, the angels who are escorting Him, in triumphant
tones address the company at the portals:

> "Lift up your heads, O ye gates;
> And be ye lift up, ye everlasting doors;
> And the King of glory shall come in."

The waiting angels at the gates inquire:

> "Who is this King of glory?"

This they say, not because they know not who He is, but
because they desire to hear the answer of exalted praise:

> "The Lord strong and mighty,
> The Lord mighty in battle.
> Lift up your heads, O ye gates;
> Even lift them up, ye everlasting doors;
> And the King of glory shall come in."

Again the waiting angels ask:

> "Who is this King of glory?"

The escorting angels reply in melodious strains:

> "The Lord of hosts,
> He is the King of glory."
> —Psalm 24: 7-10.

Then the portals of the city of God are opened wide, and the angelic throng sweep through the gates amid a burst of rapturous music.

All the heavenly host are waiting to honor their returned Commander. They wait for Him to take His place upon the throne of the Father.

But He cannot yet receive the coronet of glory and the royal robe. He has a request to present before the Father concerning His chosen ones on the earth. He cannot accept honor till before the heavenly universe His church shall be justified and accepted.

He asks that where He is, there His people may be. If He is to have glory, they must share it with Him. Those who suffer with Him on the earth must reign with Him in His kingdom.

For this Christ pleads for His church. He identifies His interests with theirs, and, with a love and constancy stronger than death, advocates the rights and titles purchased by His blood.

The Father's answer to this appeal goes forth in the proclamation:

"Let all the angels of God worship Him." Hebrews 1:6.

Joyfully the leaders of the heavenly host adore the Redeemer. The innumerable company of angels bow before Him, and the courts of Heaven echo and re-echo with the glad shout:

"Worthy is the Lamb that was slain to receive power, and riches, and wisdom, and strength, and honor, and glory, and blessing." Revelation 5:12.

Christ's followers are "accepted in the Beloved." In the presence of the heavenly host, the Father has ratified the covenant made with Christ, that He will receive repentant and obedient men, and will love them even as He loves His Son. Where the Redeemer is, there the redeemed shall be.

The Son of God has triumphed over the prince of darkness, and conquered death and sin. Heaven rings with voices in lofty strains proclaiming:

"Blessing, and honor, and glory, and power, be unto Him that sitteth upon the throne, and unto the Lamb for ever and ever." Revelation 5:13.

Coming Again

OUR SAVIOUR is coming again. Before parting with His disciples on the earth, He Himself gave them the promise of His return.

"Let not your heart be troubled," He said. "In My Father's house are many mansions: . . . I go to prepare a place for you, And if I go and prepare a place for you, I will come again, and receive you unto myself; that where I am, there ye may be also." John 14:1-3.

He did not leave them in doubt as to the manner of His coming. "The Son of man shall come in His glory, and all the holy angels with Him, then shall He sit upon the throne of His glory: and before Him shall be gathered all nations." Matthew 25:31, 32.

Carefully He warned them against deception: "If they shall say unto you, Behold, He is in the desert; go not forth: behold, He is in the secret chambers; believe it not. For as the lightning cometh out of the east, and shineth even unto the west; so shall also the coming of the Son of man be." Matthew 24:26, 27.

This warning is for us. Today false teachers are saying, "Behold, He is in the desert," and thousands have gone forth into the desert, hoping to find Christ.

CLYDE PROVONSHA

True to His promise, Jesus will come again to take all His waiting children with Him back to heaven. His coming will be the grandest and most awful sight that human eyes have ever seen.

And thousands who claim to hold communion with the spirits of the dead are declaring, "Behold, He is in the secret chambers." This is the very claim that Spiritualism makes.

But Christ says, "Believe it not. For as the lightning cometh out of the east, and shineth even unto the west; so shall also the coming of the Son of man be."

At Christ's ascension the angels declared to the disciples that He would "so come in like manner" as they had seen Him go into Heaven. Acts 1:11. He ascended bodily, and they saw Him as He left them and was received by the cloud. He will return on a great white cloud, and "every eye shall see Him." Revelation 1:7.

The exact day and hour of His coming has not been revealed. Christ told His disciples that He Himself could not make known the day or the hour of His second appearing. But He mentioned certain events by which they might know when His coming was near.

"There shall be signs," He said, "in the sun, and in the moon, and in the stars." Luke 21:25. And He speaks still more plainly: "The sun shall be darkened, and the moon shall not give her light, and the stars shall fall from heaven." Matthew 24:29.

Upon the earth, He said, there shall be "distress of nations, with perplexity; the sea and the waves roaring; men's hearts failing them for fear, and for looking after those things which are coming on the earth." Luke 21:25, 26.

"And they shall see the Son of man coming in the clouds of heaven with power and great glory. And He shall send His angels with a great sound of a trumpet, and they shall gather together His elect from the four winds, from one end of heaven to the other." Matthew 24:30, 31.

The Saviour adds: "Now learn a parable of the fig tree; when his branch is yet tender, and putteth forth leaves, ye know that summer is nigh: so likewise ye, when ye shall see all these things, know that it is near, even at the doors." Matthew 24:32, 33.

Christ has given signs of His coming. He says that we may know when He is near, even at the doors. When the trees put forth their leaves in the spring, we know that summer is near. Just so surely, when the signs appear in the sun and the moon and the stars, we are to know that Christ's coming is near.

These signs have appeared. On May 19, 1780, the sun was darkened. That day is known in history as "the dark day." In the eastern part of North America, so great was the darkness that in many places the people had to light candles at noonday. And until after midnight the moon, though at its full, gave no light. Many believed that the day of judgment had come. No satisfactory reason for the unnatural darkness has ever been given, except the reason found in the words of Christ. The darkening of the sun and the moon was a sign of His coming.

November 13, 1833, there was the most wonderful display of falling stars ever beheld by men. Again thousands believed that the day of judgment had come.

Since that time earthquakes, tempests, tidal waves, pestilence, famine, and destructions by fire and flood, have multiplied. All these, and "distress of nations, with perplexity," declare that the Lord's coming is near.

Of those who beheld these signs He says, "This generation shall not pass, till all these things be fulfilled.

Heaven and earth shall pass away, but *My* words shall not pass away." Matthew 24:34, 35.

"The Lord Himself shall descend from heaven with a shout, with the voice of the Archangel, and with the trump of God: and the dead in Christ shall rise first: then we which are alive and remain shall be caught up together with them in the clouds, to meet the Lord in the air: and so shall we ever be with the Lord. Wherefore comfort one another with these words." 1 Thessalonians 4:16-18.

Christ is coming, coming with clouds and with great glory. A multitude of shining angels will attend Him. He will come to raise the dead, and to change the living saints from glory to glory.

He will come to honor those who have loved Him and kept His commandments, and to take them to Himself. He has not forgotten them nor His promise.

There will be a relinking of the family chain. When we look upon our dead, we may think of the morning when the trump of God shall sound, when the "dead shall be raised incorruptible, and we shall be changed." 1 Corinthians 15:52.

That time is near. A little while, and we shall see the King in His beauty. A little while, and He will wipe all tears from our eyes. A little while, and He will present us "faultless before the presence of His glory with exceeding joy." Jude 24.

Wherefore when He gave the signs of His coming He said, "When these things begin to come to pass, then look up, and lift up your heads; for your redemption draweth nigh." Luke 21:28.

12

The Lord warned Lot of the impending destruction of Sodom, and because Lot heeded the warning, he was saved.

A Day of Judgment

THE DAY of Christ's coming is a day of judgment upon the world.

The Scriptures declare, "Behold, the Lord cometh with ten thousands of His saints, to execute judgment upon all." Jude 14.

"Before Him shall be gathered all nations: and He shall separate them one from another, as a shepherd divideth his sheep from the goats." Matthew 25:32.

But before that day, God warns men of what is coming. He has always given men warning of coming judgments. Some believed the warning and obeyed the word of God. These escaped the judgments that fell upon the disobedient and unbelieving.

Before He destroyed the world by a flood, God commanded Noah, "Come thou and all thy house into the ark; for thee have I seen righteous before Me." Genesis 7:1. Noah obeyed and was saved. Before the destruction of Sodom, angels brought to Lot the message, "Up, get you out of this place; for the Lord will destroy this city." Genesis 19:14. Lot heeded the warning and was saved.

179

So now we are warned of Christ's second coming and of the destruction that is to fall upon the world, and all who heed the warning will be saved.

The righteous, as they behold Christ at His coming, will exclaim, "Lo, this is our God; we have waited for Him, and He will save us." Isaiah 25:9.

Because we know not the exact time of His coming we are commanded to watch. "Blessed are those servants whom the Lord when He cometh shall find watching." Luke 12:37.

Those who watch for the Lord's coming are not to wait in idleness. The expectation of Christ's coming is to make men fear God's judgments upon transgression. It is to awaken them to repentance for their sins in breaking His commandments.

While we watch for the Lord's coming, we are to be diligently working. To know that He is at the door, should lead us to work more earnestly for the salvation of our fellow men. As Noah gave the warning from God to the people before the flood, so all who understand the word of God are to give warning to the people of this time.

"But as the days of Noe were, so shall also the coming of the Son of man be. For as in the days that were before the flood they were eating and drinking, marrying and giving in marriage, until the day that Noe entered into the ark, and knew not until the flood came, and took them all away; so shall also the coming of the Son of man be." Matthew 24:37-39.

The people of Noah's day abused the gifts of God. Their eating and drinking led to gluttony and drunkenness.

They forgot God, and gave themselves up to every vile and abominable deed.

"God saw that the wickedness of man was great in the earth, and that every imagination of the thoughts of his heart was only evil continually." Genesis 6:5. It was because of their wickedness that the people of that time were destroyed.

Men are doing the same things today. Gluttony, intemperance, untamable passions, evil practices, are filling the earth with wickedness.

In Noah's day the world was destroyed by water. God's word teaches that it is now to be destroyed by fire.

"By the word of God, . . . the world that then was, being overflowed with water, perished: but the heavens and the earth, which are now, by the same word are kept in store, reserved unto fire against the day of judgment and perdition of ungodly men." 2 Peter 3:5-7.

The people before the flood mocked at God's warnings. They called Noah a fanatic and alarmist. Great and learned men declared that such a flood of waters as he foretold had never been known, and that it would never come.

Today God's word is little heeded. Men laugh at its warnings. Multitudes are saying, "All things continue as they were from the beginning of the world. There is nothing to fear."

At this very time, destruction is coming. While men ask in scorn, "Where is the promise of His coming?" the signs are fulfilling.

"When they shall say, Peace and safety; then sudden destruction cometh upon them; . . . and they shall not escape." 1 Thessalonians 5:3.

Christ declares: "If therefore thou shalt not watch, I will come on thee as a thief, and thou shalt not know what hour I will come upon thee." Revelation 3:3.

Today men are still taken up with eating and drinking, planting and building, marrying and giving in marriage. Merchants are still buying and selling. Men are contending for the highest place. Pleasure lovers are crowding to theaters, horse races, gambling hells. Everywhere excitement prevails; yet the day of probation is fast closing, and the door of mercy is soon to be forever shut.

For us were spoken the Saviour's words of warning:

"Take heed to yourselves, lest at any time your hearts be overcharged with surfeiting, and drunkenness, and cares of this life, and so that day come upon you unawares." Luke 21:34.

"Watch ye therefore, and pray always, that ye may be accounted worthy to escape all these things that shall come to pass, and to stand before the Son of man." Luke 21:36.

The Home of the Saved

*T*HE DAY of Christ's coming is a day of destruction only to evil. It is a day of redemption, not only for God's people, but for the earth.

God created the earth to be man's home. Here Adam dwelt in that garden of delight which the Creator Himself had beautified. Though sin has marred God's work, yet the human race has not been abandoned by its Creator; nor His purpose for the earth set aside.

To this earth angels have come, with the message of redemption, and its hills and valleys have echoed their songs of rejoicing. Its soil has been trodden by the feet of the Son of God. And for more than six thousand years, in its forms of beauty and gifts for sustenance, the earth has borne witness of the Creator's love.

This same earth, freed from the curse of sin, is to be man's eternal home. Of the earth the Scripture says, that God "created it not in vain, He formed it to be inhabited." Isaiah 45:18. And "whatsoever God doeth, it shall be for ever." Ecclesiastes 3:14.

So in the Sermon on the Mount the Saviour declared, "Blessed are the meek: for they shall inherit the earth." Matthew 5:5.

So the psalmist long before had written, "The meek shall inherit the earth; and shall delight themselves in the abundance of peace." Psalm 37:11.

With this agree the words of the Scripture, "The righteous shall be recompensed in the earth." They "shall inherit the land, and dwell therein for ever." Proverbs 11:31; Psalm 37:29.

The fires of the last day are to destroy "the heavens and the earth, which are now;" but there shall come forth "new heavens and a new earth." 2 Peter 3:7, 13. The heavens and the earth will be made new.

"Eye hath not seen, nor ear heard, neither have entered into the heart of man, the things which God hath prepared for them that love Him." 1 Corinthians 2:9.

No human language can fully describe the reward of the righteous. It will be known only to those who behold it. We can not comprehend the glory of the Paradise of God.

Yet we have glimpses of that land even now; for "God hath revealed them unto us by His Spirit." 1 Corinthians 2:10. Precious to our hearts are the pictures of that country which the Bible gives.

There the heavenly Shepherd leads His flock to fountains of living waters. The tree of life yields its fruit every month, and the leaves of the tree are for the service of the nations.

There are ever-flowing streams, clear as crystal, and beside them waving trees cast their shadows upon the paths

Joys of the New Earth

The earth made new will be a lovely and beautiful place. All trace of sin and death will be forever gone, and only love and happiness and peace will be there for the saved to enjoy through all eternity.

PAINTING BY ROBERT T. AYRES

prepared for the ransomed of the Lord. There the wide-spreading plains swell into hills of beauty, and the mountains of God rear their lofty summits. On those peaceful plains, beside those living streams, God's people, so long pilgrims and wanderers, shall find a home.

"My people shall dwell in a peaceable habitation, and in sure dwellings, and in quiet resting places." "Violence shall no more be heard in thy land, wasting nor destruction within thy borders; but thou shalt call thy walls Salvation, and thy gates Praise." Isaiah 32:18; 60:18.

"They shall build houses, and inhabit them; and they shall plant vineyards, and eat the fruit of them. They shall not build, and another inhabit; they shall not plant, and another eat: . . . mine elect shall long enjoy the work of their hands." Isaiah 65:21, 22.

There, "the wilderness and the solitary place shall be glad for them; and the desert shall rejoice, and blossom as the rose." "Instead of the thorn shall come up the fir tree, and instead of the briar shall come up the myrtle tree." Isaiah 35:1; 55:13.

"The wolf also shall dwell with the lamb, and the leopard shall lie down with the kid; . . . and a little child shall lead them." "They shall not hurt nor destroy in all my holy mountain," saith the Lord. Isaiah 11:6, 9.

There will be no more tears, no funeral trains, no badges of mourning. "There shall be no more death, neither sorrow, nor crying, . . . for the former things are passed away." "The inhabitant shall not say, I am sick: the people that dwell therein shall be forgiven their iniquity." Revelation 21:4; Isaiah 33:24.

There is the New Jerusalem, the capital of the glorified

new earth, "a crown of glory in the hand of the Lord, and a royal diadem in the hand of thy God." Her light is "like unto a stone most precious, even like a jasper stone, clear as crystal." "The nations of them which are saved shall walk in the light of it: and the kings of the earth do bring their glory and honor into it." Isaiah 62:3; Revelation 21:11, 24.

The Lord says, "I will rejoice in Jerusalem, and joy in My people." "The tabernacle of God is with men, and He will dwell with them, and they shall be His people, and God Himself shall be with them, and be their God." Isaiah 65:19; Revelation 21:3.

In the earth made new, only righteousness shall dwell. "There shall in no wise enter into it any thing that defileth, neither whatsoever worketh abomination, or maketh a lie." Revelation 21:27.

God's holy law will be honored by all beneath the sun. Those who have proved themselves true to God by keeping His commandments, shall dwell with Him.

"In their mouth was found no guile." "These are they which came out of great tribulation, and have washed their robes, and made them white in the blood of the Lamb. Therefore are they before the throne of God, and serve Him day and night in His temple." Revelation 14:5; 7:14, 15.

————

"The statutes of the Lord are right, . . . and in keeping of them is great reward." Psalm 19:8-11.

"Blessed are they that do His commandments, that they may have right to the tree of life, and may enter in through the gates into the city." Revelation 22:14.

Jesus loved and blessed the children. He told His disciples, "Suffer little children to come unto Me and forbid them not, for of such is the kingdom of heaven."

Blessing the Children

"The Master has come over Jordan,"
    Said Hannah, the mother, one day;
"He is healing the people who throng Him
    With the touch of His finger, they say.
And now I shall carry the children,
    Little Samuel, and Rachel, and John,
I shall carry the baby Esther
    For the Lord to look upon."

The father looked at her kindly
    But he shook his head and smiled:
"Now who but a doting mother
    Would think of a thing so wild?
If the children were tortured with demons,
    Or burning with fever, 'twere well,
Or had they the taint of the leper
    Like many in Israel."

"Nay, do not hinder me, Nathan;
    I feel such a burden of care.
If I carry it to the Saviour,
    Perhaps I can leave it there.
If He lay His hands on the children,
    My heart will grow lighter, I know,
And a blessing forever and ever
    Will follow them as they go."

So over the hills of Judah,
 Along by the vine-rows green,
With Esther asleep on her bosom,
 And Rachel her brothers between,
'Mid the throng who hung on His teaching
 Or waited His touch or His word,
'Mid the row of proud Pharisees bending
 She pressed to the side of the Lord.

"Now why shouldst thou trouble the Master,"
 Said Peter, "with children like these?
Seest not how from morning till even
 He teacheth and healeth disease?"
Then Christ said, "Forbid not the children,
 Permit them to come unto Me,"
And He took in His arms little Esther,
 And Rachel He set on His knee.

And the heavy heart of the mother
 Was lifted all earth-care above,
And He laid His hands on the brothers,
 And blessed them with tenderest love:
And He said of the babes in His bosom,
 "Of such is the kingdom of heaven";
And strength for each duty and trial
 That hour to her spirit was given.

                    —Selected.

Behold the
Lamb of God,
which taketh away
the sin of the world.

John 1:29